Hello Liebling Haus

Photo Essay by Yael Schmidt

Original Wooden Door, Entrance

Original Fish Pond, Entrance

Idelson Street

Living in The City – The School Program

Open for Renovation

Crafts and architecture students who helped with the renovation of the wooden elements.

HOW TO - Courses for Adults

The Max & Tony Studio

Doing: Thinking
Classes for Children

Workshops & Courses for Adults

First Floor

Reception

The Permanent Exhibition

Exceptional: The White City - an Everyday Heritage

First Floor

Conservation as Culture

White City Time line

A Great Place To Live

Architecture is Frozen Music

The Project Space
Changing Exhibitions

Matters of Conservation

The Urban field Manifesto

First Floor

Cafe and Bookshop

Cafe Performance

The Garden

The Lift

Second Floor

The City Planning Lounge

Conference Room

Work Spaces
The Research Lab

The Apartment: HaDira

The Residence Program at Liebling Haus

The Scheur Family Apartment

Residency Exhibition

Home Building Program

Residency Exhibition

The Urban Artistic Hosting Platform (UAHP), Ha'Dira Exhibition

Residency Exhibition

Heritage Protection and The Common Good

Third Floor

Residency Exhibition:
The Tranfer Agreements: Transferenbau

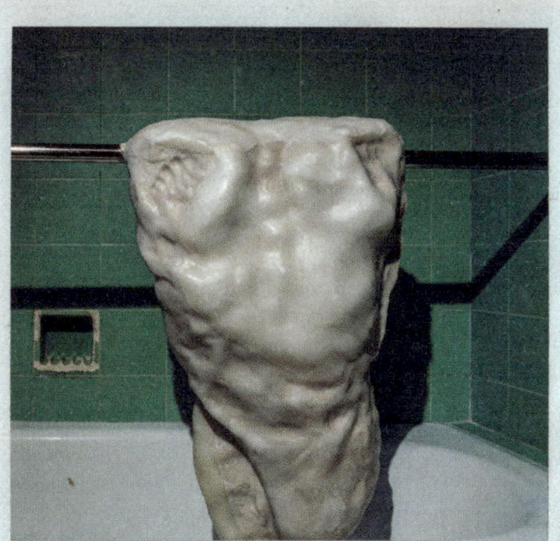

Residency Exhibition
Apartment: Réverie

Residency Exhibition
Apartment: Réverie

Exhibition Spaces

Tony & Max Liebling Apartment

Residency Exhibition: The Block

Residency Exhibition
Home Building Program

Interior, Exhibition

Third Floor

Frankfurt Kitchen

Performance
Frankfurt Kitchen – Serves You Right

Residency Exhibition
The Architecture of Optimism

Events on the Rooftop

The Fifth Space

The Rooftop

Back Staircase

Sharon Golan
Ellen Kugler
Shira Levy Benyemini
(eds.)

THE LIEBLING HAUS

Editorial direction:
Florian Heilmeyer
Katrin Voermanek

jovis

TODAY

YESTERDAY

TOMORROW

36

70

150

THE LIEBLING HAUS TODAY

THE LIEBLING HAUS YESTERDAY

THE LIEBLING HAUS TOMORROW

Sören Bartol

Parliamentary state secretary to the German federal minister for housing, urban development and building

It is a jewel in the middle of the White City. A place of rest in a city that seems like it never sleeps. A living embodiment of International Style. A trendy meeting place for citizens and travelers alike, who can relax in the cool shade of the Liebling garden. A center for heritage conservation, for urbanism and *Baukultur*, for architecture and exhibitions, a magnet for those who build things and create culture, for universities and scholars, companies, and craftspeople. It is so much more than just a building. It is the beating heart of our Israeli-German project; it has a soul and serves as a vital locus of inspiration.

It is no museum, but a living site where strategies for heritage conservation and future-focused urban development are advanced through dialogue, enabling two-way transfers of knowledge. It is here, in numerous meetings of the advisory board and board of trustees, where we have had passionate discussions together, seeking and finding a way to carefully renovate the building while preserving its historic value. We have grown in tandem with the structure.

The German government is proud to have found, in the Liebling Haus, new ways to cooperate with the city of Tel Aviv-Yafo and the Tel Aviv Foundation, and to have created a location where people can come together. The result is a place that fosters thought, that radiates ideas for approaching the structures of classical modernism throughout the city. The project was officially launched in 2015 to mark the fiftieth anniversary of diplomatic relations between Israel and Germany, following preparatory meetings that had been held since the 2010s.

On every floor in the Liebling Haus, behind every door and at every landing in every set of stairs, visitors can immerse themselves in the shared architectural past of Germany and Israel. Here, German master craftspersons and journeyworkers came together with Israeli students and trade specialists to work on carpentry, plaster, and paint, to laugh, drink, and eat. Each bit of work undertaken during the renovation was an act of communication between nations.

Together, we made the Liebling Haus fit for its opening in the Bauhaus year 2019. Since then, it has become a lively forum for Israeli-German discussions and an integral part of the city's everyday life.

Thank you, Liebling!

Udi Carmely

City engineer of the municipality of Tel Aviv-Yafo

Tel Aviv-Yafo's slogan is the "nonstop city"—and indeed the city is in constant flux. A vast amount of construction and infrastructure works is taking place all over the city, from the refurbishment of its historic heart to the erection of high-rises at its fringes, while underneath it all, a tunnel is being dug for the light rail. New cycling paths, too, are being marked out all around to create sustainable transport and enhance spaces for pedestrians, including many new public areas.

The Liebling Haus was originally established in 2019 as a visiting card for the UNESCO World Heritage Site, nominated in 2003 because of its many Bauhaus buildings and the historic urban landscape of Sir Patrick Geddes's Garden City plan. The center was established as a collaboration and partnership between Tel Aviv-Yafo and the German government as ongoing support to maintain the joint heritage of the site, which was built mainly by German Jews who had fled the country in the fifth immigration wave, using German know-how and building traditions.

Since its inauguration, however, the Liebling Haus has managed to become much more than just a visiting card for tourists eager to engage with the city's heritage. It has also developed into a platform for the professional community that actively involves citizens in the discourse of city planning and architecture. In this role, it serves to highlight, educate, and present urban topics, disseminating knowledge in the form of education courses for children, exhibitions, professional seminars, and tourist tours, while strengthening Israeli-German collaboration.

In short, the center has developed into an urban cultural hub with a unique flair that invites creators from multiple disciplines to take part in activities or spend time in the Liebling's public spaces. As the city as an urban space continues to evolve and transform, issues of civic engagement, cultural sustainability, and ecological planning have come to be essential to its strategic agenda. I see the Liebling Haus as playing an important part in actively promoting public awareness—in its identity with the city's historic cultural heritage, on the one hand, and in its future resilience and ability to continuously adapt to the rapid transformations of our era, on the other.

Ellen Kugler

Department head, White City Tel Aviv Office,
Rhineland-Palatinate Office for Federal Construction

Berlin, December 2012. Israeli Prime Minister Benjamin Netanyahu and German Chancellor Angela Merkel meet during the fourth Israeli-German Intergovernmental Consultations, with results published on St. Nicholas Day: it is announced that the German Federal Ministry of Building and stakeholders in Tel Aviv intend to cooperate in researching, documenting, and conserving the modernist buildings of the Israeli metropolis. Their ambitious goal: to "conserve and restore the White City of Tel Aviv." The lighthouse project White City Tel Aviv/Center for Architecture and Heritage Conservation is born as an Israeli-German collaboration between the Ministry of Building, the City of Tel Aviv-Yafo, and the Tel Aviv Foundation.

This book seeks to describe this unique collaborative project, trace the knowledge gained by its participants, and look both back into history and forward into the future—while also not forgetting the world today. The German Federal Ministry of Building has provided project funding of three million euros for the period from 2015 to 2025; the Israeli funding goes beyond that because of ongoing building maintenance.

The White City of Tel Aviv has been a UNESCO World Heritage Site since 2003 and includes some 3,700 buildings. Influenced by the Bauhaus style, it is the world's largest ensemble of classical modernist architecture. It was built in the 1930s and 1940s by Jewish architects, as a modern residential district for the numerous emigrants and refugees from Europe. The White City is closely linked to the fate of German and European architects of Jewish faith who were expelled from Germany after 1933.

The year 1919 saw the founding of the Bauhaus, an art school established by Walter Gropius in Weimar; it was closed after the Nazi rise to power in 1933. Among the Jews who began to flee Germany for Mandatory Palestine were some architects who brought the formal language developed at the Bauhaus to Tel Aviv.

Under the direction of the architect Sharon Golan, the Liebling Haus was successfully renovated as a collaborative trades project, opening its doors for the 100th anniversary of the Bauhaus in 2019 as an educational center and site for exhibitions, readings, and other projects. Today, it is a fixture in Tel Aviv and has been led since 2016 by Director Shira Levy Benyemini, who brought extensive knowledge and experience from her work in preserving the White City and in urban planning. Future topics for the collaboration include questions such as: How will it be possible to create affordable urban housing? How can we inspire those interested in building renovations to conserve valuable architecture in compliance with historical protection laws, while also advancing energy efficiency? And how can sustainable urban development be achieved?

How many founding mothers and fathers can a network, an idea, or a building tolerate? One thing is certain: the Liebling Haus has many parents. Friends, companions, committed politicians, enthusiastic architects, researchers, and learners worked with talented craftspersons to turn the Liebling Haus into a place of learning and thinking in the heart of the White City in Tel Aviv.

Sharon Golan, today the Lab director of the Liebling Haus, laid the foundation for the bilateral project in 2012 through tireless lobbying efforts. At the time, she was working as a heritage conservation architect in Tel Aviv-Yafo. Born in the Upper Palatinate, Golan is well-connected and speaks perfect German, a stroke of luck for the ambitious project. Together with Reinhold Robbe, at the time the president of the German-Israeli Society in Berlin, she successfully advocated for the project in Germany.

For the year 2012, which is considered the birth year of the project, the following founding supporters should be mentioned in addition to Golan and Robbe: the art historian and professor Regina Stephan; the architect Winfried Brenne; Jeremie Hoffmann, head of the Conservation Authority in Tel Aviv; Professor Jörg Haspel, at the time the state conservator in Berlin; Günther Hoffmann, head of the Construction Department in the German Federal Ministry of Building; and department head Matthias Vollmer. The state secretaries Gunther Adler, Marco Wanderwitz, Volkmar Vogel, and Sören Bartol have consistently put their heart and soul into the success of the project as members of the board of trustees.

Many clever people worked together on the advisory board and board of trustees. To keep this introduction short, their names and those of the members of the changing teams in Germany and Israel are listed in the appendix of the book. The project participants have experienced exciting, tumultuous, and inspiring times. Of course, there were some tensions: everyone was pushing hard to work together and find the best possible ideas and results; the process was always lively and passionate, yet also straightforward. We learned a lot with and from each other and are united in knowing that the Liebling Haus has come of age—and that it will continue to experiment with what it can achieve, to grow and thrive.

To life, Liebling!

THE

LIEBLING

HAUS

TODAY

What is the Liebling Haus in Tel Aviv? How was this building transformed from a residence into a cultural center for research, exhibitions, and meetings on urbanism, architecture, and conservation? And what role has Germany played in this transformation? What parts of the past can visitors still see and feel? What else can be learned about the city's heritage from the spaces of the house, and how does learning take place in a center that is constantly seeking to experience and learn?

“WE ALWAYS WANT TO MAKE CONNECTIONS TO CONTEMPORARY ISSUES.”

Working hand in hand: Shira Levy Benyemini (left) and Sharon Golan

In conversation with Katrin Voermanek, **Shira Levy Benyemini**, cofounder, director, and artistic director of the Liebling Haus, and **Sharon Golan**, initiator and cofounder of the center, and director of the Liebling Lab, talk about the projects' origins and the thematic priorities they are pursuing with their program.

What is the Liebling Haus today? And how much does it have to do with you personally and with your professional background?
Shira Levy Benyemini: You could say that our entire program, all of its content and various formats, can be traced back to our time in the building when it was still empty. Sharon and I set up our workspaces and started developing the idea for a visitor center. Initially, we were asked to think of a rather traditional information and visitor center. But during our time here—as temporary users, so to speak—we came to better understand the building and realized that it can also be something else entirely. We invited Hila Cohen-Schneiderman to work with us on a residency program for ten creators and created something resembling a think tank. Together with people from all kinds of disciplines, we thought about how we could use this building to help tell the story of the White City.

Shira, you have studied the subject of temporary building use, right?
SLB: Yes. I had no experience before that or knowledge on how to run such a place in practice. But I had done intensive research on how it's possible to activate vacant buildings through temporary use: old public buildings, synagogues, industrial buildings, through a strategy of studying the place and determining the right development for it. First, I did this as an independent study, and later for the city with a team of advisors, together with the strategic planning unit. At the time, there were nearly 250 empty buildings in Tel Aviv owned by the municipality. Today, the city has a dedicated department with its own employees just for this issue, within the culture office. For me, the Liebling Haus was an ideal opportunity to examine under favorable conditions the possibility of turning a residential building into a public one, by translating theoretical concepts into practice. Along with my experience in conservation programs and exploring the conflicts in the field of urbanism, I realized that the temporary use of the house can help in understanding the real needs of the area and formulating a proper development strategy for the place.

Sharon Golan: My story begins a bit differently. I was born in Germany but grew up in Tel Aviv, then studied architecture at IIT in Chicago,

Mies Van der Rohe's school after departing from Germany during the war. After that, I went to study in Berlin and then returned to Tel Aviv. Somehow my destiny evolved around the Bauhaus spirit. Before my studies, I had no idea of how unique and well thought-out the city planning of Tel Aviv had been and just how outstanding its vernacular architecture was, just how many modern buildings there are with a distinctive local style. So I continued my studies with a focus on local heritage conservation to better understand the space I was about to serve. Soon enough, I started working at the city's conservation department, where I supervised numerous projects in conservation and building additions.

When the idea of establishing a center for heritage conservation came up, it was my research for a suitable site that first made me aware of the Liebling Haus. My German-Israeli background helped me to understand the bilateral aspect of this shared heritage, and so the path led via the German-Israeli Society to a connection in the German government. This is how the Israeli-German collaboration came into being that sustains the building today.

For me, the whole renovation process was extremely important, especially the ethical dimension of being able to tell the story of the building and its inhabitants as part of the conservation process. What do we rebuild, what do we need to repair, how do we uncover its historic layers, and what do we make visible so that this structure showcases best practices as an exemplary historical renovation? We had to discuss and decide this question again and again as it applied to numerous details. At the same time, with the support of the city and our advisory board, we developed the content program bit by bit, and thanks to my colleague Shira a strong emphasis on community was part of the project from its inauguration.

SLB: We always had Tony Liebling in the back of our minds—she wanted this building, which she had built together with her husband Max, to be dedicated to culture and education. That was our most important goal.

At first, we worked conventionally, developing a program centered on different spaces: 100 square meters for a library, 100 square meters for a café .... But that didn't lead to anything that would have really been convincing as a concept. And that left even more space for the process of temporary use to change the whole spirit of the project. It became clear to us that a center for different communities had to be created here—a place where the neighborhood could come together, as could various disciplines related to art, design, and architecture. We created a dialogue with people from universities in the city, as well as practicing architects, and they all told us that there is no such place in Tel Aviv and in Israel. The individual museums sometimes had thematic exhibitions, they added, but a center where an open discourse could develop was missing. We decided that the Liebling Haus would be this place.

So it was clear that the White City would play a role, as would the International Style architecture, the Bauhaus influence, and Germany in general. But that was by no means all of it. We wanted to create a place for research and strategic thinking about historical and contemporary issues across the city, a place that would also be relevant for universities. Today the Liebling Haus is an open space for discussions on widely different topics of architecture and urbanism. And that's why we moved

"White City Center" into the second part of our name. There are so many areas in the city that demographically and geographically are not identified as a part of the White City, and we didn't want to exclude them from the outset.

How did you find the issues you wanted to address?

SLB: We realized we could find essential things we should be studying and exhibiting right here in the building, without looking any further. The first thing that came up was the idea for the Open for Renovation program, which over time became more extensive (see pp. 53ff) and gave the entire renovation process public visibility. I thought it would be a great opportunity to take this challenge of the renovation and to create it as the main theme of the year. Within this framework, we also began to explore the Liebling Haus and its materials. For instance, via the tiles in the stairwell we became aware of topics such as the transfer agreement (see pp. 80ff). At first, what we were doing together with the Bauhaus Dessau Foundation and the artists from our residency program was more an artistic than a scholarly investigation. But through the technical discussion regarding this agreement, this investigation later got a lot of things going.

SG: We realized something else that would be important here, something we already came across while working for the city's heritage conservation department—and we are, after all, something like the extended arm of the municipal administration. We wanted to create a better understanding of what heritage conservation means, as well as more appreciation and awareness for how one should treat the valuable existing buildings and urban structure, while using stuff at hand and not necessarily replacing parts. The aim was to showcase the beauty of the historic building—not only for guests from outside the city, but especially for the residents of Tel Aviv themselves. So education was to be given a place, and specifically a kind of education that starts with children and the neighborhood community. It is from here, then, that the essential building blocks that characterize the Haus today emerged: exhibitions, research, and education while constantly merging conservation and a holistic approach of sustainable city planning.

SLB: Because the basis for the center was nevertheless the legacy of modernist architecture, we decided to create the permanent exhibition *Exceptional: The White City—An Everyday Heritage*, which deals with the history of the city and the building from this point of view. In conjunction with the exhibition, curated by Sabrina Cegla and Hadas Zemer Ben-Ari, we created an audio guide based on many stops in the city (curated and directed by Lia Kohavi), and a painted map of the city on the rooftop terrace to complete this local, place-based perspective. In addition, on the first floor there is a project room which further develops the question "What is a White City?" and, in fact, leaves the end of the permanent exhibition open. The center also features a gallery for regularly changing exhibitions that include contributions from guests in our residency program HaDira, which translates as "the apartment."

In this program, we explore concepts related to living in the city through the space of an apartment. Although the artists do not live in the center, they can use the apartments for their exhibitions. We also have a library and coworking spaces aimed at learning and developing shared materials as part of the research lab; there is also the city planning lounge, and a research lab; used for research about the city, its architecture and the life it harbors. To support this work, the Lab also networks with other institutions and serves a resource for applied research carried out by Tel Aviv's departments for heritage conservation, planning, and sustainability. The city planning lounge space, which complements the Liebling Lab, allows us to provide access to city plans, policy documents, and studies that are at the forefront of the city's planning. A significant layer in the center's educational and pedagogic work is the School of the City, created and managed by the architect Eran Eizenhamer. In the school, we offer courses and workshops for children and adults plus seminars and city tours based on a unique program inspired by the Bauhaus institutions (see p. 61ff).

And the café is the fourth building block that brings the community together?

SLB: The café is another important reason that people come to the Liebling Haus. After all, Tel Aviv is a city where sitting in a café is a big deal. People meet here, neighbors come, some work here, parents pass their time while their kids are in the open studio. It was important to us that a manager in the café would be a part of the place. For example, Itamar Wiener, who founded Café Lev/Heart Café at the house, also creates activities and content that combines music and art, and we have worked with him closely. Even before he opened the café he used to come here with his daughter, and got to know and to love the place. In this way, the people of the café and its visitors are exposed to the building and its story. Eventually, it was clear to us from the beginning that the café is an inseparable part of the house as a whole, as is the garden, where many of the café's visitors sit and are exposed to the vegetation that is based on Geddes's plan.

What is the significance of the Liebling Haus today? Why is it important for Tel Aviv now, five years after it opened?

SLB: There is an open invitation here to slow down and linger in the moment. Tel Aviv calls itself the "nonstop city." Whether you think that's good or not—it's true in any case that everything is constantly changing, and everywhere something new is popping up. We are used to the change and this pace, but actually we also want to put down roots. Or at least pause for a moment. And that's what this new place is for. The pace is different here; things are calmer. And anyone can come here—the professional community, the neighborhood, residents, anyone interested really, adults and children—to understand their own life in Tel Aviv a little better, whether they come to the garden, the café, an exhibition, an event, or the roof terrace.

Can other institutions or "slower" cities learn something from the Liebling Haus project? Is there anything they can adopt?

SLB: On many issues, Tel Aviv is a kind of laboratory for developments that are also taking place in other places in Israel and, beyond that, in Germany and Europe. Cities almost everywhere in fact share the same problems, and we are just a few years ahead of other places in terms of many things that are happening. I think we have found a good way here of taking up topics, presenting them, and facilitating open discussions. Yes, I think some of what we are doing can be applied elsewhere.

SG: Tel Aviv-Yafo is currently under an immense amount of stress resulting from extreme number of new building constructions and renovations, as well as expanded infrastructure and gentrification. The resulting social inequality, plus extreme hot weather conditions, might serve as a fast-forward testing lab for other metropolitan areas which will face similar problems of climate change in the future.

We are not an example of a museum where you push buttons to access information. We don't just want to exhibit things; we also want to generate knowledge and challenge our visitors to think about and gain an awareness of space. When they visit, they are allowed to find their own way through the building, to move freely. There is an audio guide, but no set course to follow. The experience should be completely different from the idea of a guided museum tour. Rather, you come to a home that welcomes friends in its living rooms.

Some guests might be surprised that the building is not a typical destination for Bauhaus pilgrims. As venerable as the outer shell may be—in the exhibitions inside guests encounter themes that are not only historical but also quite current: climate change, urban gardening, modern art and installations relating to the public space. How do you set your priorities?

SG: We certainly see our task as appreciating the site's historical heritage and communicating its values. But always, we're trying to build a connection to contemporary issues and see what we can learn from the past given the many challenges our cities are currently facing. It is important to us to communicate about urban planning and architecture in ways that allow lay people to understand the issues and actively participate in the discussions, as members of civil society. Ultimately, the urban landscape and the spaces we live in impact the well-being of us all. As residents, this is something we all need to do together. As for priorities, we feel that conservation lets us look at history and learn from the past how to deal with contemporary issues. The privilege of being a multidisciplinary center between the municipality and academic and professional crowds lets us feel the pulse of the city and get inspired by the subjects that arise from the ground up.

SLB: We currently have four major thematic areas that determine our program. First, there is the holistic, participatory idea of the Garden City for Tel Aviv, which can be traced to Patrick Geddes and his urban development plan (see pp. 74ff) and which we take up again and again in various ways, as with the *By Leaves We Live* project and the *Urban Bloc Gardens* exhibition. We started *By Leaves We Live* in 2018 at the Venice Architecture Biennale together with AN+ Architects from Tel Aviv and the Department of Architecture at the Bezalel Academy of Arts and Design. We simply decided to publish the text that Geddes wrote for the city's master plan while deeply engaging with the idea of an urban utopia as a shared habitat for people and plants, which also led to a publication. In addition, *By Leaves We Live* was presented at the 2018 Venice Architecture Biennale as part of the Ideal Spaces Working Group's "Artificial Natures" symposium. The Geddes Plan will be one hundred years old in 2025, and we will devote a lot of space to this anniversary.

The second major topic centers on the persistent conflicts between conservation and development around the buildings in the White City, which has been a UNESCO World Heritage Site since 2003. How can this modern heritage avoid being turned into a museum and be kept alive as a living space for the people who reside here? One important project was certainly the international competition Layer 2.0, which we initiated in 2021, with the winners chosen in 2022 by a prominent Israeli-German jury; the aim was to find new designs for adding additional storeys to International Style buildings (see p. 49f and pp. 86ff).

The third major theme is the public space in Tel Aviv. We held a large exhibition, *Welcome to the Re:Public Haus*, that presented the theme through artworks exploring the idea through the spaces in the house, and works dealing with the actual public space outside. A fourth topic that concerns us is the theme of community as a necessary urban component—whether on the large scale of urban society, in the form of neighborhoods, within an apartment block, in a shared building, or around a community garden. In this context, we are carrying out activities that also aim to work with the communities at various scales. When I say community, I also mean the community that is re-created time and again when we hold events here at the Liebling Haus.

↑ Clemens Haury (on the left), director of the Liebling Haus project at the German Federal Ministry for Housing, Urban Development and Building, in conversation with Eran Eizenhamer, director and curator of the education program School of the City.
↓ Moran Navon, the center's content manager at "The Whispering Weeds," an evening at the exhibition *The Urban Field Manifesto*, curated by architect Sabrina Cegla

"WE FELT THAT WE NEEDED SOMETHING LIKE THE LIEBLING HAUS, NOT TO PROVIDE ANSWERS, BUT TO ALLOW US TO ASK QUESTIONS."

Jeremie Hoffmann says few projects have as many parents as the Liebling Haus. As head of the heritage conservation department in Tel Aviv-Yafo, he was directly involved in the center's founding, and he now still provides support and counsel as a member of its board of trustees. In this interview with Katrin Voermanek, he talks about interaction, openness for experimenting, and the Liebling Haus as a model for other institutions.

When visitors come to the Liebling Haus, Sharon Golan often greets them by saying: "This city is not a museum; it's a place where we live. This building is not a museum; it's a site that we use. We want people to come and use it, too." As the city's chief officer for heritage conservation, can you unpack that a little bit? How can you conserve something valuable by not turning it into a museum but by opening it up to everyday use?
I would expand on Sharon's statement and say: the building is not a museum; it is something like a psychoanalyst's couch. It is a place where you can become aware of yourself. We believe that a good city needs such a place in order to ask questions about its history and its future, a place to try to reread history and use what is discovered to move forward into the future. Being here is a kind of time-out in the city's development process.

Our idea of conservation is an attempt to look at ourselves. That's before we even get to any grand narratives about the Bauhaus or modernism. First, we try to look at and understand our local narrative. Everything is changing so rapidly that we hardly have time to ask ourselves who we are. This building then can be the therapy couch where we lie down not to solve problems and get answers, but to ask questions and look at a process. And this is a process that never comes to a conclusion.

People used to think that heritage conservation could provide answers. There were globally recognized approaches to conserving buildings, guidelines on how to handle materials, and so on. But it's like the way it is in medicine: the more we know, the clearer it becomes that there can be no single set of rules for solving problems at all, simply because problems have different causes at multiple levels. When we established the department for heritage conservation, we felt that we needed something like the Liebling Haus, to provide a place for all our open questions.

When was that?
This process began in the mid-1990s, when my predecessor Nitza Metzger-Szmuk was leading the department, not me. At that time, it consisted of two people. Later, when I became the second director in 2005, there was a desire for a grand plan to guide the conservation of the city center—in other words, for ideas of what should be done with the White City, and with

city's brutalist and postmodernist heritage. Today, our focus is on the sustainability of our modern heritage. But for all of these issues, the main thing is know-how for deciding what to conserve, why, where, and how much. And to allow us to better explore these topics, to have a better connection with the city, with its people—homeowners, artists, researchers, children, senior citizens—we wanted to create a place, initially just a building, without immediately giving it a label. For us, the Liebling Haus is the heart of it all, a place where people can feel at home. It is an open house, an urban house for the city. Residents come here and reconsider what they think or know about the city by asking questions. In the Liebling Haus, in other words, we're always trying to foster interactions—and that's another belated answer to your first question.

One thing you immediately notice is just how visible the renovation process is in this building. You can see layers from different periods of time everywhere; old and new overlap or encounter each other. It seems anything but perfect, which perhaps runs counter to the expectation that many visitors have when they walk into a "Bauhaus heritage building." Where does this principle of revealing processes while also leaving space for things that are unfinished come from?

Honestly, it's the result of a dilemma. When we started working on this building, we knew that we would become a model for the city. Because one thing is obvious: if the heritage conservation department renovates a historic building, it better be more than perfect. And yet we also knew that we could never create anything perfect; it's pointless to even try. So we asked ourselves: What is good? Not: What is perfect? How can we realize this project in a way that also illustrates our approach to heritage conservation? For starters, one of our most important skills is adapting quickly. We are also able to make solid, long-term plans, but here things change overnight. This agility does not mean disorder: it's just a different kind of order. It is very efficient, and indispensable, because otherwise we would not survive as a country.

And personally, I don't believe in such a thing as perfect conservation, in the more conventional attempt to immaculately restore buildings. This approach is not even something people in Israel can really relate to: we are a society of immigrants, and for generations there was never any attachment to buildings. What there always has been is an attachment to texts and philosophical ideas. Only recently has something new been added to this. People are now spending money not just on cars, but also on residential architecture and on making it high-quality. Something like a culture of residential architecture is emerging. I have the feeling that a revolution is taking place. This generation is completely changing the way people think about their homes and the value of the local environment.

Does all this apply only to the special conditions here in Israel and in Tel Aviv? Or can we learn something in Germany, in Europe, or elsewhere from the Liebling Haus—can we learn something about heritage conservation and debates surrounding it?

I am quite sure that anyone and everyone can learn a lot here. Let's make a comparison to a museum: there, the curator is considered the smartest person in his field. They decide what counts as the best work of art by a particular artist, which then goes into the exhibition. And in principle, that's fine. But that is only *one* way of doing things.

Another way, which is what we are proposing here, is the idea of a more open structure. Let's talk about which works of an artist or group influence us. Let's transform visitors into active participants. When I go to a museum today, my position is a passive one. I'm not allowed to touch anything, I'm not allowed to talk out loud, I'm not allowed to comment on things. I'm not allowed to do anything, except to come in, look, and then leave.

Our idea is for an open platform. And yet this absolutely doesn't mean that we aren't contributing ideas of our own. We're not pretending that we let visitors decide everything. The strategy is rather to present clear ideas for discussion. What we want is a back and forth. Sometimes we give the lectures and expect others to listen to us; other times we just listen and try to be as open as possible. What matters to us is not having control over the results, but over the process. This always comes at a price, because what we can control is more limited. But this also means that we gain a lot.

Are the visitors able to engage well with this kind of openness?
Sometimes at the beginning, you experience a kind of shock, because the Liebling Haus is not what you expect. We tend to compare what we perceive with what we already know, and this is true, as well, when you visit a public institution: you compare it to all the other public institutions you've visited. Places where the walls are, generally speaking, neatly painted. Here, they are not. But you can also get used to this new experience and realize that it's not a problem at all, but emblematic of a kind of discussion, of a different way of looking at things—and of a certain idea that is already becoming more widespread. I am suddenly seeing new restaurants with walls that are also left unpainted. We've drawn attention to brutalism, and all of a sudden we see buildings where the plaster is being removed to uncover and reveal the reinforced concrete. A whole new aesthetic is developing. And this making visible of layers fits the DNA of Tel Aviv as a city.

It is remarkable how much historic conservation in Tel Aviv has to do with the essence of the city, especially, of course, with regard to the White City. We're not just talking here about a few individual properties or a small housing estate, but about an entire urban fabric. And when you ask how we ought to deal with architectural heritage, you are also asking about the entire city and its future development. In Tel Aviv, housing is scarce, and there's a lot of pressure—how is the city dealing with this?
It's true, UNESCO has recognized the entire core area of the city, with over 3,700 structures, as a World Heritage Site. It is one of the few places where you can see how the modern idea of the Garden City was implemented in reality. And here, too, it's the case that if we want to preserve the city as a place to live, we can't just conserve it, but have to think beyond that. That is why we have allowed extra storeys to be added to the buildings.

It's inconceivable that someone would suggest this for Stuttgart's Weißenhof Estate ...
That we are doing it here has to do with the fact that, unlike in other countries, there is no government funding for renovations in Israel.

There is no help or financial support from the state or the government to maintain buildings. So cities have to find their own solutions. Moreover, Tel Aviv cannot continue to grow outward. There are no open spaces, except for a small area to the north, but even that is already under construction. So the city has to grow within the existing architecture, and that's why we made the decision that 80 percent of the historic buildings could be expanded with a two- or three-storey addition.

Since when has this been allowed?

There was no specific point in time; rather it was a process in the 1980s and 1990s. The situation here is that owners who lose building rights due to historic conservation orders are entitled to compensation. A city might be able to do that with one building or a handful of them—but here we're talking about hundreds. Huge sums of money would have been involved. So we decided to create a new level in the city. And, fortunately, it was possible to align this with the principles of UNESCO, which understands that cities need to adapt to change. And that brings us back to the idea of layers and the initial question: we have renovated the Liebling Haus in a way that allows you to see the layers of time that overlap here. And we don't just tell visitors about it: we want them to see, touch, and feel these layers. The layers are walls. Yet they also stand for worlds that have disappeared. So it's about showing things that no longer exist, but have left traces we can talk about. This is our most important message: "Let's talk about it ... What do all of you think about it? What does each of you think about it individually?" This building is an open code.

You can hardly be better prepared for the future. What do you think it will it bring, for the Liebling Haus and for Tel Aviv?

What's happening right now with Artificial Intelligence is, I think, the greatest revolution of all time. We should deal with this proactively, and I am trying to encourage my employees to do so, as well. Regardless, I firmly believe that a city is an organic, living system, and that it will become increasingly important for people to understand their city as part of a holistic approach to life. So hopefully they'll be less and less inclined to constantly destroy and rebuild things. Hopefully, we will return to the insight that existing structures have value and that we should preserve them not for conservation reasons, but simply because they are there. Like with our body: even if the doctor were to say—"OK, your arm is broken, let's take it off and make a new arm out of some fantastic, innovative metal"—you would never do it! Instead, you would try to live with what you have. Hopefully, this will also be the case for buildings and cities. And I hope, I imagine, that the Liebling Haus will be a leader in this process.

OPEN FOR RENOVATION:

THE BUILDING AS A SITE FOR KNOWLEDGE EXCHANGE AND ENCOUNTERS

An architect, exhibition designer, and curator, Sabrina Cegla has been part of the Liebling Haus's founding team since 2015, coformulating the center's vision and values. As senior curator at the Liebling Haus, she has initiated and curated numerous projects, including the permanent exhibition. Here she describes the Open for Renovation project, which was coconceived and directed together with Sharon Golan. Based on Cegla's curatorial concept and design for the project, the Liebling Haus was transformed into a performative-educational construction site, inviting visitors to participate and discuss the process, even before the building officially opened.

Usually when a building is under construction, it is closed for renovation, left standing shut down and divorced from its natural surroundings until it is reborn in a new version of itself. Often, construction sites create noise and dust pollution in the neighborhood, unsurprisingly provoking resentment among nearby residents. Since the Liebling Haus wanted to reach out to the community and invite it to be part of the site from the very start, we decided to turn this introverted process around by making it into an extraverted one.

Open for Renovation was a multidisciplinary project that ran from 2017 to 2019, focused on the conservation and renovation of the Liebling Haus. It transformed the building into an open urban site of collective production, knowledge exchange, and encounters and aimed to

↑ German students from Knobelsdorff-Schule (Berlin) during a window workshop, led by zukunftsgeraeusche
↓ An evening with serenades and encounters on the subject of balconies as part of Open for Renovation

↑ Ready-to-wear helmets designed for the Open for Renovation tours
↓ Installation in a Liebling Haus bathroom by artist Naama Bar Or

showcase the process as a live architectural performance and laboratoy, inviting the professional and general public to take part, explore, and discuss topics of conservation, maintenance, and repair, while seeing and feeling the site from within. The building foremost became an "educational construction site," a *Bauhütte* (a historical term describing a tradition of a joint building effort by artisans in large-scale construction projects, housed in a lodge or workshop on site) for German and Israeli masters and apprentices aspiring to revive shared traditional historical building crafts and promote craftsmanship. A significant part of the modern building tradition came to Israel from Germany in the 1930s and much of it had been lost over the years due to different circumstances, such as the fact that Israel has no official vocational training programs for craftspersons. Encounters among young apprentices from the same field enabled a broad cultural exchange.

On-site workshops focused on restoration and maintenance instead of replacing various building elements, enabling the participants to take part in the actual process of restoring the building while negotiating hands-on conservation approaches relevant to the local restoration agenda. On-site tours for the public led by the architects, designers, craftspeople, and engineers involved in the project discussed aspects of the practical and ethical side of the conservation process and the difference between renovation and maintenance, asking specifically what should be saved, what should be repaired, and what should be replaced. Lectures by historians, sociologists, architects, and artists focused on the various rooms of the building's apartments, discussing everyday life and the cultural values incorporated in their physical design. The lectures were accompanied by performances, screenings, site-specific art installations, and interventions. By exposing the building during its physical, spatial, functional, and programmatic transition from a residential to a public site, the project offered an opportunity to examine how modern architecture continues to influence and shape our living spaces and environment to this very day.

Open for Renovation was an Israeli-German bilateral investigation that revived a shared material culture heritage. It enabled new perspectives on modern architecture through first-hand experiences on site, while exploring the essence of the International Style in Tel Aviv in a way that stretched beyond aesthetic values to incorporate history, technology, identity, and culture. The project challenged conventional conservation practices by proposing a new way of approaching restoration: as an opportunity for shared learning, experimentation, and exchange of knowledge beyond the boundaries of professional expertise.

In 2018, the project was invited to participate in a conservation fair in Leipzig, Germany. In the absence of the main subject—the building itself—the exhibition offered a fragmented view. The focus lay on the materiality of the building, on the crafts incorporated in it, on building elements, and on the events held during the renovation, which were reminiscent of a forgotten shared *Baukultur* (a wholistic view of construction that emphasizes the integration of architectural design, urban planning, and artistic elements in creating spaces). The exhibition revealed the complexity of the architectural act and the forces acting on it.

The program has proposed a new model for architectural conservation and education, by emphasizing the importance of craftsmanship, collaboration, and community engagement in the process of building renovation. It reconnected the building to its urban heritage and to present-day city life, while laying a foundation for a sustainable future by rethinking the ideas of conservation, maintenance, and repair as everyday social, cultural, and environmental practices.

Our partners for this project hailed from both the academic and professional sectors: Knobelsdorff-Schule and Max-Bill-Schule, Berlin, Handwerkskammer Berlin, zukunftsgeraeusche TU Berlin, Sto Foundation, Keimfarben, Arco, Brenne Architekten, Shenkar College, Bauhaus-Universität Weimar, Etz Ladat, and others.

The Sto Foundation was particularly involved in the Open for Renovation project, providing generous financial support and enabling young apprentices from Germany in plasterwork and painting to spend one week each in Tel Aviv, where they were able to practice their craft under Israeli-German guidance and in exchange with local young colleagues at the Liebling Haus construction site. At the end of the exchange, they were allowed to tour and become more familiar with their host country as part of a three-day cultural program. The Sto Foundation provided media coverage of the project and published detailed documentation on its website.

The QR code leads directly to the Sto Foundation website.

Installation by the artist group TAPETHAT during a month dedicated to the living room as part of Open for Renovation

SCHOOL OF THE CITY:

INSPIRED BY THE BAUHAUS SCHOOL

Shira Levy Benyemini introduces the School of the City, the Liebling Haus's educational program, with its wealth of offerings designed to encourage the perception, understanding, and exploration of the built environment.

The School of the City, founded and led by architect Eran Eizenhamer, is a space inside the Liebling Haus for doing, experimenting, and creative thinking. It offers a wide range of programs for adults and children, inspired by the Bauhaus School, and developed and taught by professional architects, artists, designers, and educators. The lessons take place in small groups in the spaces adjusted for that all over the house.

In the workshops, School of the City promotes creative, multidisciplinary thinking that recognizes the city as a space for learning, inspiration, and multisensory ingenuity. We believe that the city offers a solid foundation for learning and creativity that drives civic engagement with where we live. The School of the City also offers classes and workshops for children who want to invent,

make, draw, plan, think creative thoughts, and better understand life in the city. Its Doing:Thinking program for children focuses on creative thinking in the spirit of the Bauhaus. The workshops are guided by the philosophy of learning by doing, a pedagogical method that provides children an opportunity to develop their skills by experimenting with various tools and materials and promoting intuitive, independent thought, self-confidence, and multidisciplinary perspectives.

The school's Olympus program is an innovative, out-of-this-world offering for young artists who have completed degrees in art, architecture, design, performance, and dance studies—for people seeking a platform to develop and refine their creative work based on principles of equality, dialogue, and collaborative creation. We focus on valuable interactions, group studies, and experimental work, attentive to each participant's individual tendencies and learning habits. There are no dull lectures or authoritarian, hierarchical evaluations at Olympus.

In all of these programs, the approach to learning emphasizes the importance of context and place in shaping our understanding of the world. By studying the space and place where lessons occur, students can develop a deeper appreciation for the ways in which our surroundings influence our experiences and shape our perceptions of the world. This helps foster a sense of curiosity and exploration, as students of every age and background learn to see the world through new eyes and discover new possibilities in familiar places. The development of ideas and study plans is always directly linked to actual learning outcomes. This means that students do not just spend their time memorizing facts or completing assignments, but are actively engaged in the learning process and encouraged to think critically and creatively about the material they are studying.

It's fascinating to see how this approach to learning is focused not only on the practical aspects of architecture and design, but also on the more intangible qualities of space and place. By exploring the qualities of light and its presence in the rooms, students are able to understand its impact on our experiences and emotions in a space. This type of observation can be very insightful, as it helps to develop a deeper appreciation for the ways in which design and architecture can influence our well-being.

Similarly, by looking at the water and electricity system connected to the building and its apartments, students are able to understand the complex systems that support our modern lives. This type of exploration can help cultivate a sense of responsibility and appreciation for the infrastructure that supports our daily activities. The language that emerges from this type of learning is also quite interesting: by expanding and contracting between feelings and metaphors, students can develop a more nuanced and poetic understanding of the world around them. And by exploring the different dimensions of space and place, they are able to develop a more holistic understanding of the world and their place within it. It's intriguing to see how this approach to education has led to the creation of a free and open conversation that lacks predefined concepts. Moving in the classroom space like phenomena moving in the world, the conversation takes on a life of its own and becomes a dynamic and immersive learning experience.

Here and on the following pages: architecture and activism workshops led by Rotem Volk

THE

LIEBLING

HAUS

YESTERDAY

What did the Liebling Haus use to be? Who had it built, and who designed it? Who used to live here? What is special about its renovation? Why were traces of alterations and additions made visible? Can this specific kind of renovation be transferred to other buildings? Why are international experts interested in this renovation? Why did so much of the building material come from the German Reich in 1936? Why and how is the Tel Aviv Bauhaus different from the German one?

ONLY BAUHAUS? MODERNISM IN TEL AVIV

A city that rose from the dunes outside Yafo, a city that never sleeps, is constantly changing; an architecture in which international and local influences have come together to create a form of modernism all its own. **Sharon Golan** summarizes the short and eventful history of Tel Aviv, introduces key players, and tells of a chance find in the Liebling Haus that opened up a new perspective on just how extensive the transfer was—not only of ideas and people, but also of materials and products—from Europe and the German Reich to Mandatory Palestine.

Driving along the Ayalon Highway into the center of Tel Aviv, one is immediately struck by the many new skyscrapers that stretch upwards amid a forest of cranes. This ring of towers encircles the historic old town almost like the rim of a giant bathtub. But the White City, the ten-hectare UNESCO World Heritage Site in the city center, is also in danger of being swallowed up by the current construction frenzy.

Tel Aviv prides itself on being a global city, a city that never sleeps. Like other cities in the "West," Tel Aviv is characterized by the contrast between its historic city center and its outskirts, which are constantly being developed, and by the conflict between believers in progress and traditionalists. The challenges of a growing city, of climate-friendly urban redevelopment, and of how to deal with the historical heritage of modernity collide here abruptly—and literally. For several years, the city has been promoting the conservation of three-storey modernist buildings by incentivizing private owners with the opportunity to add two or three additional floors in return for implementing conservation measures. This is currently generating a very specific type of construction aimed at increasing the density of the city center, creating what is almost a second level of the city, a de facto layering of new construction on top of the historic buildings. This concept stems from the tension between wanting to conserve important cultural features of the city and the urgent need to create housing. It thus represents an economic compromise, balancing the needs of both conservation and densification. Through it all, the 115-year-old city is striving to adapt to Israel's hectic lifestyle as a "start-up nation."

And even if Tel Aviv has long been considered a Bauhaus city: from a scholarly perspective, the architecture of the White City belongs to the International Style, a term introduced in 1932 by the architectural theorist Henry-Russell Hitchcock and the architect Philip C. Johnson. It denotes a design approach that was contemporary at the time and stands for unadorned, functional architecture. The International Style shaped modern European architecture from the 1920s onward, spreading from there to the world. In Tel Aviv, it was an expression of the young city's desire to appear as modern as possible. At the same time, the intention was to deliberately create a new architectural environment. It was intended to provide a counterpoint to the building traditions in the countries where the many immigrants had come from, and to the local architectural style of the Levant.

In common parlance, "Bauhaus" has become synonymous with International Style in Tel Aviv—not least because it conveys a powerful advertising message that is also associated with the luster of having realized a social utopia. And yet the architecture of the city is too complex to be simply called Bauhaus style. It combines numerous theories and influences from various protagonists of modernism. Among the most prominent influences visible in the cityscape are certainly Erich Mendelsohn's dynamically curved functionalism, Le Corbusier's five design principles of modern architecture, and the moderate modernism of figures such as Henry van de Velde, the cofounder of the Werkbund. His ideas reached Israel in its early days through architects such as Dov Karmi, who had studied with van de Velde in Belgium. From all these influences, Tel Aviv developed its own "glocal" architectural style: influenced by European impulses, but adapted to the given climatic and cultural conditions.

Beginnings

The origin of the White City lies in the Geddes Plan: in 1925, the British, who had administered the region as a mandate since 1920, commissioned the Scottish urban planner Sir Patrick Geddes to implement new urban planning ideas in Mandatory Palestine. Originally a botanist and geologist, Geddes was a progressive urban planner and urban ecologist familiar with local conditions. In 1919, he was commissioned to develop a master plan for the Hebrew University in Jerusalem. Although the design was not realized, it had a major influence on future urban planning. He proposed turning Tel Aviv into a Garden City based on the ideas of British urban planner Ebenezer Howard. Following this ecological approach in combination with his own definition of the city as a continually changing organism, Geddes developed a plan that combined independent buildings organized in a large block with a garden in the center to serve the residents of the block. One basic principle was to admit light and air into the structures and to allow the streets to be ventilated by the wind blowing from the sea, which was accomplished by creating small gardens and open spaces around the detached houses, together with first floors elevated on pilotis (one of the five architectural principles envisioned by Corbusier). Geddes laid out a hierarchical structure for the road network consisting of main thoroughfares, residential streets, and footpaths.

Allenby Street, view toward the Mediterranean, 1924

Rothschild Boulevard, newly constructed, on a postcard from the 1920s. View of the intersection with Herzl Street, with the Mediterranean Sea in in the background and the old town of Yafo on the left edge.

General Development Plan for Tel Aviv from 1931, directly modeled on the Geddes Plan of 1927

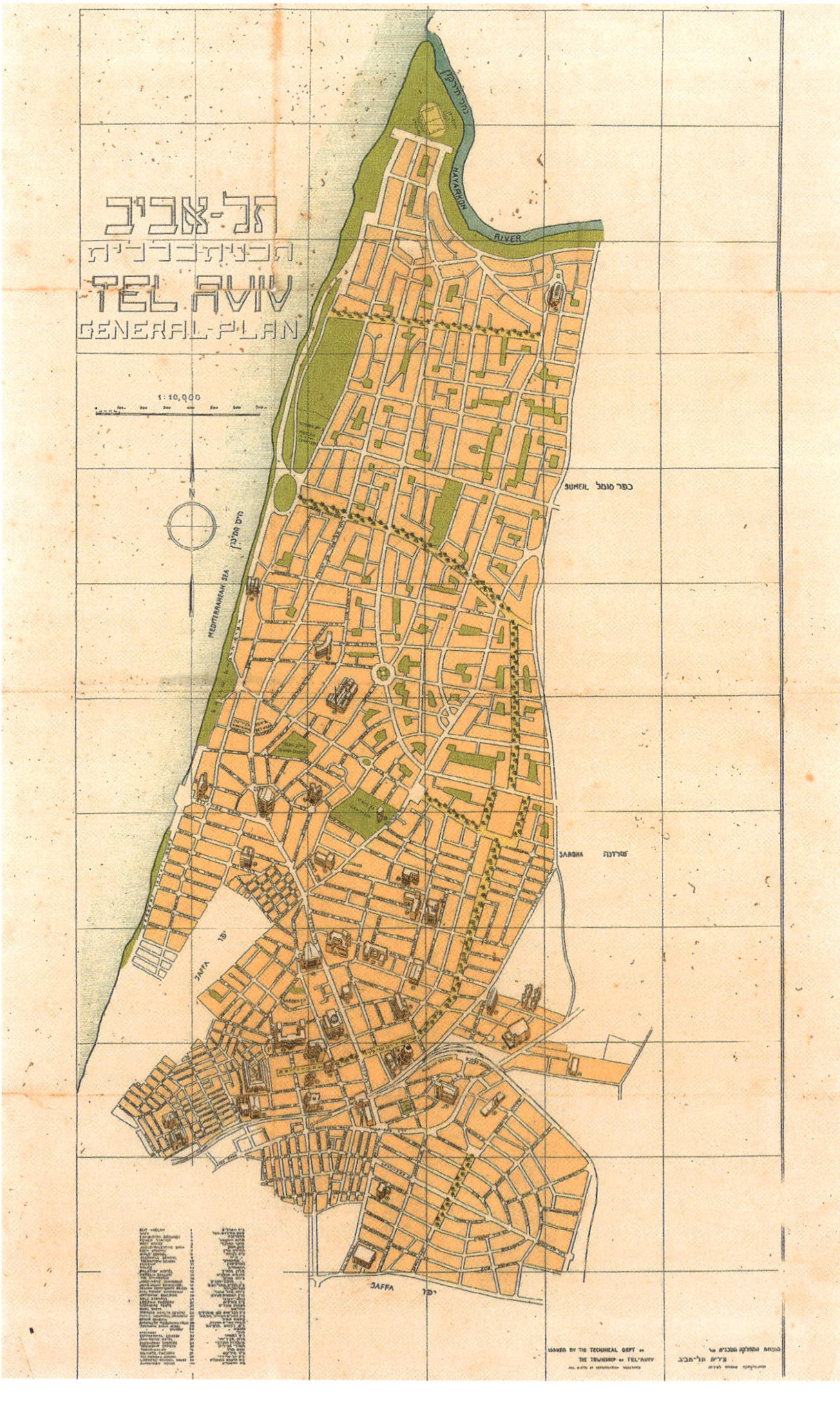

His visionary design, completed by 1925, aspired to be more than just an urban master plan: it was intended as a political, social, and cultural tool with the goal of developing an ideal living environment for the new Jew. This human engineering was a crucial, ideal building block for those in the Zionist movement who dreamed of rebuilding a proud Maccabean nation. The Zionists believed that this goal could be achieved through measures that included resettling the emigrants from the Eastern European ghettos in a healthy, green, Garden City—in other words, in a livable environment that would satisfy both physical and spiritual needs. Yet no one would have dreamed that the young city, founded just outside the city walls of the ancient port of Yafo, would see such massive growth in such a short time: between 1932 and 1938—especially after the Nazis came to power in Germany in 1933—around 200,000 European Jews fled to Mandatory Palestine. During this period, the population of Tel Aviv tripled to about 150,000, rendering many of Geddes's original ideas obsolete. As a result, some of them were modified, but the main principles were integrated into the design in a way that was adapted to the urban reality.

Built by tens of thousands of immigrants, Tel Aviv is a melting pot of cultures cast in International Style concrete silhouettes. The city has no outstanding icons of architectural history to speak of, nor are there any independent architectural Bauhaus masterpieces recognized as such. There is thus a lack of architecture that could, by itself, define the style of the city. What gives the White City its outstanding cultural significance is rather the fusion of its structures with the urban environment, that is to say, with the historic urban landscape, which extends far beyond the boundaries of the area declared a World Heritage Site. The White City, including its surroundings, is a living urban fabric that is still changing today—and it should be understood as such.

The modernist building phase in Tel Aviv lasted only about six years, from 1931 to 1937. After that, the British Mandate government, responding to the Arab uprising and the increasing violence against Jews in Mandatory Palestine, ended the wave of immigration of European Jews. The heyday of the International Style and the Bauhaus movement in Tel Aviv was thus brief. Nevertheless, the influence of European architecture from the interwar period, together with new local developments, produced diverse articulations of modernism that were sensitive to both social and cultural needs.

White Modernism showcasing and symbolizing the new city of Tel Aviv, here as a collage on the cover page of the Tel Aviv city newsletter (*News bulletin of the Tel Aviv city administration*), 1935

Tel Aviv was predominantly shaped by a group of young architects who had studied in Germany, France, Belgium, Italy, and Russia in the workshops and the schools of the most famous architects of the avant-garde. Arieh Sharon, Shmuel Mestechkin, Shlomo Bernstein, Munio Gitai Weinraub, and Chanan Frenkel apprenticed at the Bauhaus, while Joseph Neufeld studied in Rome, Bruno Taut in Königsberg, Ze'ev Rechter with Erich Mendelsohn in Berlin, and Samuel Barkai with Le Corbusier in Paris. Dov Karmi, Benjamin Anekstein, Genia Awerbuch, and numerous others learned their craft in Rome, Ghent, Venice, or Naples, and later also in Vienna and Paris. Many of them became important architects in what would become the State of Israel. Their views were shaped by modernism and the prevailing zeitgeist of the time, and they were all united by the desire to give their convictions concrete form in the newly founded state.

Under the name Chug—the Hebrew translation for the Berlin architects' association Der Ring—some of them established a kind of urban think tank. This group of young visionaries included Arieh Sharon, Erich Mendelsohn, Leo Adler, Joshua Steinbock, and the architecture critic Julius Posener. Borrowing from European avant-garde circles such as the Crystal Chain or the Werkbund, Chug sought to influence the development of a modern architectural language in Israel. The goal was to find a unified, simple form of expression for the Zionist movement, with a new architectural style that would bridge the cultural differences of all Jews who immigrated to Mandatory Palestine. The construction of modernity was to be synonymous with that of the country itself: building such architecture or living in such an apartment meant being an equal among equals in every respect. While modernism thus gained new momentum in Mandatory Palestine, in Germany the movement of Neues Bauen (New Building or New Objectivity) was denounced as being "Jewish-Bolshevik" or "Semitic-Oriental"—the Weißenhofsiedlung in Stuttgart, for instance, was vilified as an "Arab village."

Aiming to influence public opinion, Chug publicized many of its ideas through formats that included a magazine, *Habinyan Bamizrach Hakarov* (Building in the Middle East), and architectural competitions, such as the one held for a new market

Arrival of White Modernism: view of the Tel Aviv promenade designed by landscape architect Avraham Karavan, 1938

hall in Haifa, won by Moshe Gerstel in 1937. Its construction is an impressive example of the New Building that Chug hoped to see in Israel. And Chug did in fact succeed in changing the aesthetics of the Yishuv—the community of Zionist Jews who had settled in Palestine since the end of the nineteenth century. The earlier stylistic eclecticism, emblematically represented by Alexander Baerwald's Technion in Haifa, came to an end, and the Zionist movement appropriated European-style modernist architecture. These structures represented the desire to create a new national identity, and modernism in Tel Aviv became a symbol of the birth of the new Hebrew nation.

Transfers

The uniform and relatively objective modern style was ideally suited to provide a roof over the heads of the thousands of Jewish refugees who immigrated to Mandatory Palestine in the 1930s. Erecting buildings with reinforced concrete frames required less time and resources than the eclectic style that had prevailed until then, with its load-bearing walls and lavish ornamentation. The solutions and concepts for construction developed by avant-garde architects in Europe proved to be appropriate for Mandatory Palestine and were readily adopted.

The most important building material, limestone for concrete production, was easily obtained locally, and processing it required no special craftsmanship. Modern construction allowed for larger wall openings, wide cantilevered balconies, and flexible interior spaces. Terrazzo could be cast with local and imported stones, while plaster was made using various processes, applying the latest techniques imported from Germany. The imitation of stone was achieved by mixing minerals such as lime and white cement with pebbles of different sizes, giving the facades a three-dimensional appearance and producing a surface that also proved to be particularly resistant to weathering. A German engineer named Emanuel Teiner once traveled to Mandatory Palestine specifically to train construction workers and teach them how to make various plaster mortars commonly used in Germany. The best example of the enormous influence of German construction techniques on the country is the fact that the German terms are still used in Israel today: *Waschputz*, *Kratzputz*, and *Steinputz*, *Oberkante*, *Unterkante*, *Sockel*, and *Stecker* are the technical terms in Hebrew for roughcast, scratch coat, aggregate plaster, top edge, bottom edge, plinth, and plug.

However, it was not only words and know-how that were imported from Germany. In 1933, the Zionist Association for Germany negotiated what has become known as the Haavara Transfer Agreement with the German Reich Ministry of Economics. This enabled Jews "willing to leave"—who were otherwise denied access to their cash assets—to transfer part of their wealth in kind to Mandatory Palestine. In return, they deposited their money in a transfer bank, where it was used to purchase machines, building materials, and other goods from Germany through the Tel Aviv–based trust company Haavara, which were then sold in Mandatory Palestine. Once the emigrants arrived in Mandatory Palestine, they were paid the proceeds of the sale less any costs incurred. The Nazi regime considered the emigration of Jews to be a stroke of luck and, facing international economic boycotts, hoped the agreement would generate foreign currency. By the beginning of the war in 1939, more than 50,000 German Jews had so managed to leave the country and escape certain death in concentration camps.

Much of the goods that came to Mandatory Palestine as a result of the agreement were used in the construction of the White City—such as tiles, glass windows, handles, and faucets, as well as metal and concrete. Many immigrants certainly used these materials not only out of longing for the European lifestyle in which they were rooted: they also wanted to display their knowledge of the latest trends in architectural design. That said, the extent to which the Haavara Transfer Agreement influenced the design and construction of Tel Aviv's White City became evident to Israelis today only through a chance discovery in the Liebling Haus: during the renovation work, a tile had come loose in the stairwell with "Villeroy & Boch, Made in Germany" on the back. We wondered how this German tile might have come to Tel Aviv. In the Zionist National Archives, I found list upon list of the German products that had reached Israel as part of the agreement with the refugees. What became clear was not only how much the design of the modernist buildings in Tel Aviv could be traced back to the transfer of ideas and people from Europe, but also the degree to which components such as door handles, washbasins, tiles, bricks, windows, etc. had come primarily from Germany. To explore this topic, we mounted an exhibition, *Transferumbau* (Transfer Rebuild) at the Liebling Haus in September 2019, which was then also shown at the Bauhaus Dessau as part of its 100th anniversary celebrations, triggering a lively discussion about the agreement in both countries.

Direct Traces of the Bauhaus

Even though there were only a few architects who studied at the Bauhaus and later built structures in Tel Aviv, the influence of this small group on architectural discourse was enormous. The Hod Cooperative Apartments, completed on Frishman Street in 1935, can be taken as an example: here, the influence of Hannes Meyer, the second, lesser-known director of the Bauhaus, is evident, both in the simple and modest lines of the design and in the social structure of the city block. Residents were assigned

View of Zina Dizengoff Square in 1939, one year after its opening. The expressive, dynamic design by architect Genia Averbuch turned the square into a central feature of the expanding White City.

From 2017 to 2018, Zina Dizengoff Square was redesigned according to plans by the local firm Moria Architects. In the 1970s, the square had become a multilevel traffic junction. Moria Architects explicitly drew on the qualities of Averbuch's original plans. The photo was taken in 2018.

only small apartments, but they shared generous communal facilities, such as a large garden in the center of the property, a kindergarten, a laundry room, several stores, and a dining hall. In keeping with the dominant socialist worldview of the elite, the common public space served as an extension of the relatively small housing units and was intended to weld the new Hebrew society into a homogeneous whole. This was precisely in line with Meyer's ideas, with slogans such as "the people's needs instead of luxury needs" and the imperative he issued to his students to focus primarily on social aspects of design.

Meyer's student Arieh Sharon, who completed his studies at the Bauhaus in 1929 with diploma no. 6, would become Israel's most important Bauhaus architect. Since Sharon had already been active in planning and construction at Kibbutz Gan Shmuel prior to his apprenticeship at the Bauhaus, it is not hard to imagine that he and his teacher quickly joined forces in a common effort to translate the ideals of socialism into architectural form. It could even be argued that the student conversely influenced his teacher, for example in the construction of the ADGB Trade Union School (for the Allgemeiner Deutscher Gewerkschaftsbund, or General German Trade Union Federation) completed in 1930 in Bernau, near Berlin. Declared a World Heritage Site in 2017, the building combines numerous features that parallel a kibbutz settlement in form and function. In both buildings, space has been designed to influence the ways in which its residents live together. At all levels—from small living spaces to semipublic spaces and large communal gathering places such as the dining hall—the architecture is designed to shape the identity of the individual as part of the group.

Sharon completed his most significant work in 1949, after the flowering of early modernism, when David Ben-Gurion, the first prime minister of Israel, commissioned him to prepare a master plan for the newly founded state. Two years later, the plan, published under the title "Physical Planning in Israel," identified the locations for new cities, industrial and agricultural land, the general system of infrastructure, national parks, and nature reserves—essentially constituting the new country's fundamental spatial planning. It's thus no exaggeration to say that Sharon, a student of the Bauhaus, was responsible not only for the design of several residential buildings in Tel Aviv, but also for the overall strategic plan for Israel itself.

The cityscape of Tel Aviv was also shaped by numerous European architects who had nothing to do with the Bauhaus, and further who had immigrated to Mandatory Palestine not out of deep Zionist convictions. Many of them had simply fled from professional bans and Nazi persecution. Although they were already established in their home countries, in Tel Aviv they now often found themselves compelled by the city architect Yaakov Shifman to adopt the International Style. Although Shifman himself was not a member of Chug, he was in constant communication with the group and shared their convictions. His gentle push for a more consistent style led to varied reactions and approaches from different architects in Tel Aviv. As they strived, with varying levels of willingness, to meet these style rules, they ended up creating many other designs, some of which were highly unique.

Perhaps the most striking feature of the local adaptation is the relationship of the architecture to the street: the buildings are in constant dialogue with their surroundings and promote social interaction between residents and passers-by. This was achieved not only by building on pilotis (as noted above) and by creating small gardens, but also by the numerous balconies. In the Mediterranean climate, these replaced the large ribbon windows characteristic of modernist buildings. They provided shaded, cool outdoor spaces for the apartments, often wrapping around the building like a sort of second skin. Together with a careful orientation of structures and streets according to the cardinal directions, this ensured improved air circulation. The balconies were also platforms for communication between neighbors and passers-by, thus fulfilling a social function as outward extensions of the living rooms. The only vertical window elements in the buildings, the "thermometer windows," were likewise conducive to this dialogue with the street: during the day they let natural light into the stairwell, and at night they in turn illuminated the street.

The White City was declared a UNESCO World Heritage Site in 2003 in recognition of its outstanding cultural significance for modernist architecture and urban planning. Today, it is considered the largest contiguous architectural ensemble built in the early International Style. It includes a total of about 3,700 buildings, of which about 1,000 are under full heritage protection and 180 are under increased protection. The Liebling Haus is one of these 180 structures.

The World Heritage Site declaration also led to a simple-sounding yet complex maintenance plan: since most buildings are privately owned, city ordinances are mainly designed to make the relatively high maintenance costs affordable for owners. Issuing building permits for adding structures to the roofs of heritage-protected buildings generates additional living space and revenue, with the proceeds specifically dedicated to covering renovation costs. That is to say: owners of historically protected buildings can finance maintenance by adding at least one floor to the building, which they then rent out or sell (at a high price). In practice, building permits can be issued for up to three floors. In addition to the requirement to renovate the existing building, additional building permits are subject to other conditions: building owners are required, for example, to make buildings more earthquake-resistant by reinforcing the existing structure; a rocket-proof shelter must also be installed, preferably in the form of a shaft in the rear of the building that cannot be seen from the front.

The planning of these additions is no easy task for architects, as building proportions were immensely significant to modernist architecture. If the extensions are built in the same style as the original building, the carefully constructed proportions of the whole risks being lost. In addition, architects are faced with the decision of whether the addition should imitate the original building or formulate a contrast to it. An imitation will blur the original design of the building beyond recognition, and yet if the extensions are built in a divergent architectural style, this new type of "upper city" might soon smother the historic buildings on the lower floors. Complicating matters further, each building in Tel Aviv has a unique character, thus making it important to carefully analyze both the original proportions and the position of the building on the lot in each case before embarking on the design of an extension.

The concept of adding storeys is likely to raise eyebrows among some conservation purists. However, the city administration is steadfastly pursuing a strategy to protect the historic city center, resisting pressure from major real estate players by

As an incentive for owners and investors to maintain historic three-storey buildings in Tel Aviv, two or three floors are allowed to be added during renovations.
Two examples of such renovations and additions: ↑ The Naparstag Heuschreck House at Rothschild Boulevard 48, converted into a hotel. The architectural firm AN+ will add a storey to the 1934 building and a glass extension at the rear. The small garden will become a public passageway with shops and restaurants. ↓ The Minzer House, also from 1934, was expanded and remodeled in 2015 for the Edmond de Rothschild Bank. Amnon Bar Or Architects added recessed glass floors on the flat roofs and inserted a connecting glass structure between the buildings.

This building (1938, architect: attributed to Robert Hoff) at Yedidya Frenkel Street was originally composed of a first floor accommodating commercial functions and two upper residential floors. It features horizontal articulations in the canopy above the first floor and the residential unit's balconies, with the balconies extending around the corner and creating a dynamic flow between the two intersecting streets. In 2017, the building was renovated by Bar Orian Architects and Mester-Gal Architects and its height raised to seven floors. The added floors differ from each other, signifying a hierarchy of importance. The first additional floor was added as an exact extension of the footprint, design, and materiality of the original floors, while the top two added floors follow the footprint while changing the materiality and architectural expression; an additional recessed rooftop floor has been placed on the roof.

approving the construction of high-rise buildings only outside the historic center, even at the risk of facing significant compensation claims from investors. The two greatest challenges to conservation thus remain the threat of natural disasters, particularly earthquakes, and the task of exploring the ways and means of promoting a positive approach that properly values conserving the cultural heritage of the White City.

Despite the flaws in the existing urban development plan, it provides apt solutions to present constraints and necessities. Israel is a very young state, just seventy-six years old, and now as ever fighting for survival. Many Israelis consider the protection of cultural heritage, especially modernism (which doesn't appeal aesthetically to everyone), to be a luxury—especially given the existential threats the country faces. Nonetheless, the existing concept respects and preserves Geddes's unique ideas and the proportions of the modern city, while enabling renewal and development. The historic heart of the city is not so privileged that it could simply become a museum; it must continue to function as the center of Israel's most important metropolis. The Liebling Haus considers its main role to be providing a platform for discussions on all these topics.

The text has been revised for this book and first appeared in German in *Aus Politik und Zeitgeschichte: Zeitschrift der Bundeszentrale für politische Bildung* 69, no. 13–14, "bauhaus" (2019).

A BRIEF HISTORY OF THE LIEBLING HAUS AND ITS RESIDENTS

THE LIEBLING HAUS

Constructed: 1936/37
Design: Architect Dov Karmi and engineer Zvi Barak
Clients: Tony and Max Liebling/Max Liebling Ltd.
Address: Idelson Street 29, Tel Aviv

The Liebling Haus was commissioned by Tony and Max Liebling. They had purchased the property on Idelson Street in early 1936, at a time when the area around Bialik Square had already become established as a quiet, upscale residential neighborhood. They had an older, eclectic building on the property demolished, allowing architect Dov Karmi and engineer Zvi Barak to design a three-storey, six-unit building. With a progressive, European upper-middle class design and floor plan, the building was intended to attract the educated, well-heeled clientele of European emigrants. The Liebling Haus can be considered a prime example of the modernist architecture built in Tel Aviv in the 1930s.

The building—the only one on the lot—is situated in such a way that the fresh air coming off the sea from the west can circulate through the living spaces and garden. Karmi structured it on the asymmetrical lot with one wing pushed backwards, creating a shaded entrance. This layout also increases the number of corner rooms and improves the ventilation of all apartments. In perfect alignment with the sea, air, and sun—the natural conditions of Tel Aviv—the building paradigmatically realizes the principles of Patrick Geddes's urban development plan. The side wing is oriented toward the sea to take maximum advantage of the westerly breeze. Each apartment has one or two balconies: in the front wing, these are long loggias facing the street, while the apartments in the rear section each have

Excerpt from an aerial map showing Allenby Street, 1949. The round Bialik Square, from which Idelson Street branches off, is clearly visible. The Liebling Haus is marked in orange.

Liebling Haus, street facade, shortly after completion in 1937

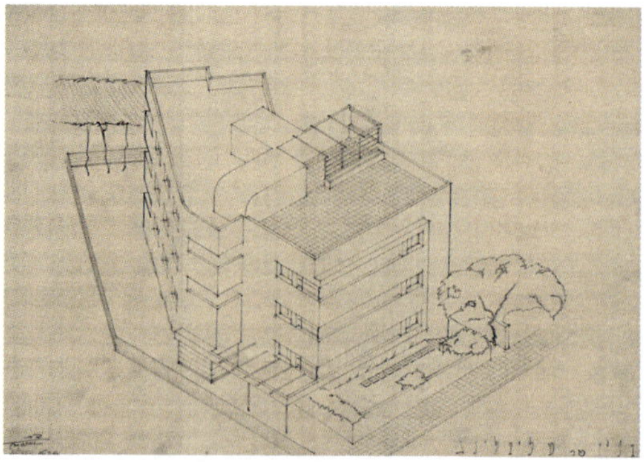

Liebling Haus, isometric view (left) and perspective view from the street (right), drawn by Dov Karmi around 1936

two smaller loggias respectively at the southern and northern ends of the building core. Comparatively small windows protect the interiors from excessive heat. Karmi replaced the ribbon windows prescribed by Le Corbusier and European modernism with street balconies that form long, horizontal lines continuing around the corners in a natural way—this could be a reference to the grand model of those years, the famous "glass corner" of the Bauhaus building in Dessau. The large rectangle, by contrast, which emerges as a relief in the plaster of the street facade and encompasses the three loggias, is based in its proportions on the golden section and thus refers to one of the oldest and most enduring doctrines of proportion in architecture.

Karmi based the floor plan design on upper-middle-class apartments in Europe. In the core of the building, he placed the staircase, compact kitchens, and bathrooms. The roof terrace and basement were shared by all residents. The entrance is located at the southwest corner and is accentuated by a pergola covered with greenery and a small water basin that provided additional cooling when the building was first constructed. The entire building is surrounded by green space. In the back inner corner, there was also a utility balcony on each floor, which was always accessible from both apartments in that area. One sign that the building was seen as an upscale residence is the fact that two floors were immediately occupied by two prominent families of doctors who had emigrated from Central Europe. As owners, the Lieblings were happy to have the rear apartment on the top floor.

Liebling Haus, entrance under the pergola, shortly after completion in 1937

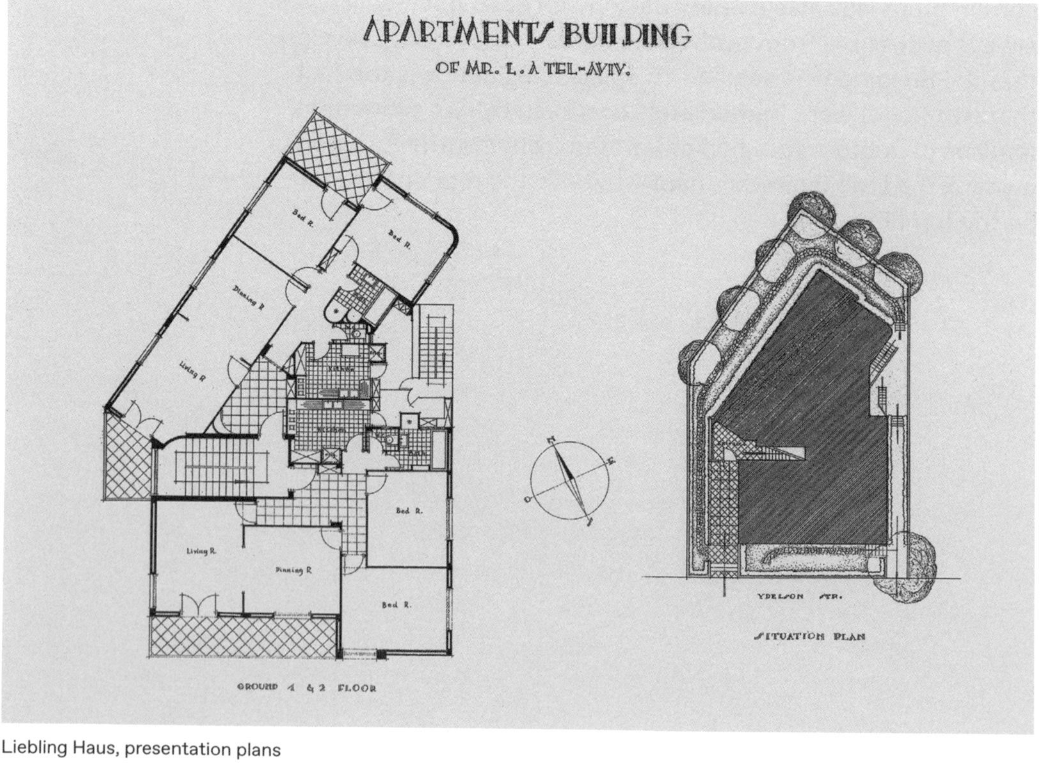

Liebling Haus, presentation plans

Liebling Haus, view of the entrance from the street, shortly after completion in 1937

THE ARCHITECT: DOV KARMI

Dov Karmi
b. 1905 in Odessa in the Russian Empire, d. 1962 in Tel Aviv

Dov Karmi came to Jerusalem in 1921, where he began to study painting at the Bezalel Academy but then switched to architecture. From 1925 to 1929, this new direction led him to the University of Ghent in Belgium, where Henry van de Velde was teaching at the time. The interplay between construction and architectural expression found in Karmi's buildings is possibly inspired by Van de Velde and Belgian art nouveau. After completing his studies, Karmi returned to Mandatory Palestine and worked for two years in the office of Meir Rubin in Jerusalem before founding his own office, Madben, in 1932. At Madben, Karmi collaborated with various partners, eventually forging a long-term partnership with engineer Zvi Barak, with whom he also planned the Liebling Haus.

In 1934, Karmi was a cofounder of the architectural and artistic group Chug (Hebrew for "ring"), which had a strong influence, through its architectural journal *Habinyan Bamizrach Hakarov* (Building in the Middle East) and the architectural competitions it organized, on the spread and acceptance of modern architecture in Israel. At the beginning of his career, Karmi primarily built private residences in Tel Aviv and the surrounding area.
In 1946, together with Ze'ev and Yaakov Rechter, he won the competition for the extension of the Cultural Center in Tel Aviv. This was followed by larger commissions such as the Histadrut office building in Tel Aviv (1949), the Zim building on Rothschild Boulevard (1950s), and an office building for the Israeli airline

Architect Dov Karmi, 1957

Dov Karmi, Dikovsky House in Ramat Gan, completed in 1934

Dov Karmi in in collaboration with Arieh Sharon, Allenby Passage in Tel Aviv, 1948–1950

Dov Karmi in collaboration with Ze'ev Rechter, cultural center in Tel Aviv, 1952–1957

El Al on Ben Yehuda Street (1956–1962). A total of some 200 buildings were constructed to his designs. Karmi was one of the best known and most influential architects in the young State of Israel. In 1957, he became the first architect to receive the Israel Prize, the country's highest cultural honor. In the 1950s, his son Ram Karmi (1931–2013) joined his father's office, as did later his daughter Ada Karmi-Melamede (b. 1936). Both Ram and Ada also became well-known architects, likewise receiving the Israel Prize. It was only in 2010, a full forty-eight years after Dov Karmi's death, that his considerable body of work was honored with an exhibition and publication.

Dov Karmi, water tower at the Afridar Center in Ashkelon, 1952

Dov Karmi, building research center on the campus of the Technion, Israel Institute of Technology in Haifa, 1955–1957

Dov Karmi, El Al high-rise on Ben Yehuda Street in Tel Aviv, 1959–1962

THE CLIENTS: TONY AND MAX LIEBLING

Tony Liebling, née Rubin
b. 1887 in Volochysk in the Russian Empire, d. 1963 in Tel Aviv
Max Liebling
b. 1881 in Pidvolochysk in the Russian Empire, d. 1942 in Tel Aviv

Tony and Max Liebling married in 1920 in Tarnopol and then moved to Switzerland, where Max had successful careers both as a merchant and in the real estate business. In 1925, the couple emigrated to Mandatory Palestine and founded Max Liebling Ltd. They acquired the property at 29 Idelson Street on 6 January 1936, and commissioned Dov Karmi to design an apartment building. Soon thereafter, in March 1937, the building was ready, and the Lieblings moved into the rear apartment on the top floor. The couple had no children. After Max's death, Tony continued to live in the apartment.

In her will, Tony Liebling bequeathed the building to the city of Tel Aviv-Yafo with the stipulation that it be used for a charitable purpose: as an orphanage, a home for the elderly or children, a student residence, or a museum. In return, all she requested was a plaque above the entrance in memory of herself and her husband. Before this could happen, however, her cousin Sarah Ruff and then their niece Sabina, along with her

Tony and Max Liebling in the 1940s

daughter Rosa, lived in the Lieblings' apartment for a time. Sabina Liebling (1908–1999) continued to reside in the apartment until 1990 and was thus the last family member in the building.

Soon after Tony's death, the city administration used some of the apartments in the building as offices. It was not until the 1990s that a kindergarten was built on the first floor. Several renovations were carried out for both the offices and the kindergarten. An initial renovation from 1997 to 1999 restored some components to their original condition, including the balconies, the wooden blinds, and the terrazzo floors of the balconies. In October 2013, when the German Federal Institute for Research on Building, Urban Affairs and Spatial Development partnered with the city of Tel Aviv to identify a location for the newly created White City Center, as it was initially to be called, the Liebling Haus was selected from among four potential sites.

ON THE FIRST FLOOR: THE MEYER FAMILY

Ludwig Ferdinand Meyer
b. 1879 in Wiesbaden, d. 1954 in Tel Aviv
Lotte Meyer, née Hertz
b. 1882, d. 1964
Daughter: Ilse

The residents of the Liebling Haus were a reflection of the young Jewish society in Tel Aviv. This was especially true of the refugees who arrived from Europe in the 1930s during the fifth aliyah. Unlike in previous waves of migration, many of those arriving this time were well-educated, intellectual, and middle-class immigrants. Many of them had already built a career in the lands they were leaving behind but found themselves forced to abandon it in the face of the growing repression against European Jews. Among the first residents in the Liebling Haus, for example, were two prominent doctors and their families.

In 1937, the renowned pediatrician Professor Ludwig Ferdinand Meyer and his wife Lotte moved to both apartments on the first floor. Ludwig had studied in Munich, Berlin, and Bonn, then worked as an assistant physician to Adalbert Czerny in Breslau and at the Charité in Berlin under Otto Heubner—both considered to be cofounders of modern pediatrics. Starting in 1918, Meyer had headed the Berlin Orphans' and Children's Home, specializing in infant nutrition. Starting from 1921, he held a full professorship in Berlin. In 1934, the Nazis forced him to resign from all official positions, and in 1936 the Meyers emigrated to Mandatory Palestine with their daughter Ilse, her husband Walter Hirsch, and their grandson Daniel, later the psychiatrist and best-selling author Daniel Offer.

In his new homeland, Meyer first worked at the Bikur Cholim hospital in Jerusalem, then at the newly built Hadassah hospital campus on Mount Scopus—a spectacularly modern design by the architect Erich Mendelsohn, who had also fled the Nazis, first to England, then to Mandatory Palestine. During his time at Hadassah, Meyer became one of the world's leading specialists in infant nutrition and metabolism.

In the front apartment facing the street, the Meyers set up a small private clinic, which they used as an apartment in the evenings; the waiting room then served as a dining room. Meyer was feted internationally for his research, and in 1953 the German Society for Pediatrics named him an honorary member. His publications were among the standard pediatric works of his time. Lotte Meyer, however, spoke little to no Hebrew until her death, conversing primarily in German, which remained the common language among the early residents of the Liebling Haus. Every Wednesday, the Meyers played bridge with the Ashermans. The Meyers resided in the Liebling Haus until Ludwig's death in 1954.

Lotte and Ludwig Meyer in their living room on the first floor of the Liebling Haus, year unknown.
The School of the City is located here today.

ON THE SECOND FLOOR: THE ASHERMAN FAMILY

Joseph Gustav Asherman (Ascherman)
b. 1889 in Rosovice in Austria-Hungary, d. 1968 in Herzliya
Malka Asherman, née Wilner
b. 1897 in Neve Tzedek, d. 1965 in Tel Aviv
Children: Nina, Juval, and Joram

Malka and Joseph Asherman moved into the second floor in 1937. Like the Meyers residing on the first floor, they occupied both apartments. Dr. Joseph Asherman was already a luminary among gynecological researchers in the 1930s and one of the most important gynecologists in the entire region. He used the apartment facing Idelson Street as a private clinic, while the family used the one in the back for themselves.

Joseph Asherman had studied in Prague and served in World War I as an officer in the Austro-Hungarian Army. He came to Palestine in 1920 at the invitation of Henrietta Szold, who had founded the Zionist women's organization Hadassah in the United States in 1912 and was in the process of establishing and improving medical care in the country. To facilitate these efforts, she invited well-known Jewish doctors and health experts from all over the world to the country. Asherman first worked as a physician in the Jezreel Valley; beginning in 1939, he founded and headed the obstetrics and gynecology ward at the newly opened Hadassah Hospital in Tel Aviv. Later he founded the Sarona Maternity Hospital, and he additionally served as a professor of medicine at the Hebrew University of Jerusalem. Asherman founded and led the Israeli Society of Obstetrics and Gynecology. He achieved worldwide fame primarily through his research on female fertility: Asherman syndrome—a groundbreaking discovery in the prevention of infertility—is named after him. Among the patients in his private clinic at the Liebling Haus was the wife of the Shah of Iran, Farah Diba Pahlavi. She received infertility treatment incognito in the 1950s and later gave birth to the long-awaited heir to the Shah. Professor Asherman worked in the maternity hospital until his last day. He died in his sleep from cardiac arrest.

Malka Asherman was born in Neve Tzedek, the first Jewish residential neighborhood in Palestine, which was established outside of the gates of Yafo in 1887 and formed the nucleus of the city of Tel Aviv. Malka was thus the only Sabra—the only Jew born in Eretz Israel—living in the Liebling Haus. Malka first studied at The Girls' School in Neve Tzedek, and then in the Herzliya Gymnasium at the beginning of Herzl Street. Later, she was active in her community, organizing Hebrew Bible studies and Hebrew language classes, especially for Jewish refugees just arriving in Tel Aviv.

The Ashermans kept an open house, full of culture. Of their three children, both sons Juval and Joram died young. Their daughter Nina volunteered for the British Army during World War II and in 1948 she married Auschwitz survivor Yehiel Feiner, who published books under the pseudonym Ka-Tzetnik (Yiddish for "concentration camp inmate"). His novels were written in an autobiographic manner that was unique at the time and gained tremendous attention worldwide. His book *House of Dolls* was translated into thirty-two languages and sold millions of copies. Upon marrying, the couple Nina and Yehiel had adopted a new and meaningful surname: De-Nur, Aramaic for "out of the fire." Feiner's family was murdered in the concentration camps, so the wedding took place as an intimate gathering in the Liebling Haus. In his book, *The Encounter*, Ka-Tzetnik describes his first visit to the Liebling Haus, even before he met Nina, noting how its beauty reminded him of his previous life in Europe.

In 1951, Nina and Yehiel had a daughter, Daniella De-Nur. While her parents stayed for long periods abroad following the tremendous success of Ka-Tzetnik's books, Daniella moved to the Liebling Haus to live with her grandparents Malka and Joseph until she was sent to the Hadassim boarding school, founded by Canadian Hadassah-WIZO, where she also graduated. Malka and Joseph resided in the Liebling Haus until Malka's sudden death in 1965—a total of almost thirty years.

Malka and Joseph Asherman flanking their daughter Nina, who proudly poses in a British uniform on the Tel Aviv promenade in 1942

Nina und Yehiel De-Nur, 3 April 1952

ON THE THIRD FLOOR: THE SCHEUER FAMILY

Eugen Mordechai Scheuer
b. 1881 in Saarbrücken, d. 1960 in Tel Aviv
Lucie Scheuer, née Weil
b. 1889 in Tübingen, d. 1978 in Tel Aviv
Children: Ruth, Hannah, and Herbert

In 1938, the Scheuer family moved with their three children into the street-facing apartment on the third floor of the Liebling Haus, while the Lieblings lived on the same floor in the back apartment facing the garden. The Scheuers faced significant challenges in leaving the German Reich, as they failed to secure the necessary visas for departure to Canada (where they had relatives) or Switzerland. They instead emigrated to Mandatory Palestine in 1936, somewhat against their will. Since they were allowed to take almost no cash, they invested their assets—reduced by the Nazis' "Reich Flight Tax"—in expensive furniture, among other things. As a result, they arrived in Tel Aviv with upper-class furnishings—including a grand piano, a large dining table for six, a heavy buffet complete with Bavarian china, and marble lampshades—which they used to furnish their modern apartment in the Liebling Haus.

In Tel Aviv, Lucie Scheuer remained a housewife and never learned Hebrew. Eugen Scheuer had worked in the flour trade in Germany, and in Tel Aviv he initially worked as a money lender. When their daughter Ruth lost her home due to bombings in the first Arab-Israeli War in 1948, she and her family sought refuge in her parents' apartment in the Liebling Haus. Lucie Scheuer resided in the building until 1971, making her the last tenant. Offices of the city administration had already moved into the lower floors. Lucie Scheuer left behind a family cookbook with recipes she had adapted for her daughter Ruth,

Here and on the following pages: three generations of the Scheuer family, in various configurations but almost always on the balcony of their third-floor apartment. All photos were taken in the 1940s.

adjusting the old German recipes to accommodate the ingredients available in Tel Aviv. This cookbook included her legendary apple strudel recipe, which was offered for a time in the new café in the Liebling Haus.

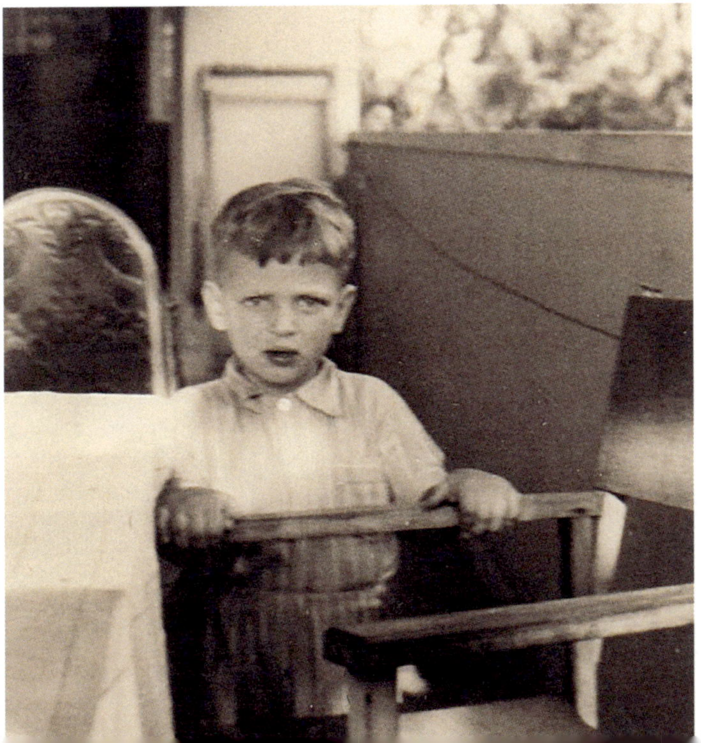

"WHEN YOU STEP CLOSE TO THE BUILDING, YOU CAN SEE THE TRACES OF HISTORY. THIS WAS SOMETHING THAT WAS VERY IMPORTANT TO US."

German architect **Winfried Brenne** and his firm specialize in renovating existing buildings, particularly those from the first half of the twentieth century—which is why he was called in as an expert for the Liebling Haus renovation, too. In conversation with Florian Heilmeyer and Katrin Voermanek, he talks about the complex issues that emerge in renovations, even in such a small residential building.

How did you come to be part of the Liebling Haus project?

I first came to Tel Aviv in the 1980s, though at that time I had no idea about the White City; the term wasn't familiar in those days. I remember being very surprised by the extent of the city's modernist heritage. In mid-2012, Sharon Golan joined our Berlin office, introduced by Sibylle Hoiman and Annemarie Jaeggi from the Bauhaus Archive, with whom we had already been working for a long time on Berlin's settlements from the 1920s. This collaboration prompted the desire to invite experts in heritage conservation from Israel to come to Germany and to deepen intellectual exchange. Eventually, this was made possible through the support of the Keimfarben company, and we organized a tour of the Bauhaus in Dessau, as well as the ADGB Trade Union School in Bernau and the six modernist housing estates in Berlin, which are collectively registered as UNESCO World Heritage Sites. Sharon worked in the Heritage Conservation Authority and made the contact with its head official, Jeremie Hoffmann. That's how we met Sharon and Jeremie Hoffmann and learned for the first time about the project for a White City Center—as the project was initially called—in Tel Aviv.

What happened next?

We got into contact again in 2014, this time via the German Ministry of Building. They suggested we submit an application for the renovation of the Liebling Haus to the Getty Foundation's "Keeping It Modern" program, which then provided funding for a comprehensive survey as the basis for the restoration. From the beginning, the Liebling Haus project was interwoven with a number of people and institutions, which didn't always make it easy. Even before we got going, there were a lot of politics in the background, despite the fact it wasn't even clear yet just what should become of the building.

Did the uncertainties regarding the programmatic focus also affect your ideas for the renovation?

Actually, no. The many discussions centered mainly on the program for the building, and not on the architecture itself. Once our application for Keeping It Modern was accepted, we had a clear mandate to conduct an in-depth analysis of the building. Our approach is tried and tested from decades of working with existing buildings. We undertake a comprehensive survey of the structure, concerned not only with the building itself but also with its urban planning and historical contexts, its history of use, and the stories of its residents, as well as conversions, additions, and technical changes. For buildings like this, we slowly work our way into the complexity. Perhaps that's why there was so little discussion about the construction project itself, because the money came from outside, which allowed us to develop a strong rationale for what needed to be done.

That said, the discussions about content and programs could certainly not be completely separately from the construction projects.
No, of course not. Since the ideas for the planed White City Center remained quite vague for a long time, it also remained unclear what spaces would be required for the new use. This is difficult for a renovation. At the same time, it was also an advantage for our work. Here, Sharon had the crucial task of incorporating the results of the inventory into the use concept. Our inventories and catalogs of measures to be taken spurred numerous discussions: What do we want to conserve? What story do we want the building to tell and how can we align that with its new use?

Walls were removed on the first floor to fit a café into the small-scale layout. And then it was decided to allow these interventions to be seen by leaving the traces of the removed walls and ceilings visible in the surfaces. There were lively discussions about whether this makes sense. Ultimately, these conversations gave rise to the idea for the Open for Renovation program: the notion that these decision-making processes at the Liebling Haus should be made public, should be put up for discussion and recommended as a model for other projects—and also that we should clearly convey that such decisions can just as easily be made differently and that all of it is a process. This has proved to be a very good, very beautiful idea.

Can you give any other examples of such decision-making processes at the Liebling Haus?
Climate and comfort are two key issues where ideas and demands have changed considerably since the building was constructed in 1936. We were particularly concerned with preventing the careless loss of original materials used in the building. We conducted an energy assessment of the building, and in this regard the Liebling Haus had undergone some significant overhauls. Not as much as in other buildings in Tel Aviv, perhaps—where the balconies, for instance, were closed off without knowing what role that would play in the building's climate. That's what our explorations are about: understanding the building as a whole. Then you understand why the orientation of the windows is important—for example, that the smaller windows face south, where the most heat is generated. The balcony railings, as well as the upper balcony aprons, always have a small slit at the bottom to allow air circulation, and the partition walls between separate living spaces have an opening at the top that can be closed, which allows for controlled air flow and thus night-time cooling. These are highly intelligent, fascinating, low-tech solutions that need to be understood to prevent them from being built over and lost, with the consequence that you then have to install an air conditioning system. These distinguishing architectural features, which spread throughout Tel Aviv in a very short time in the 1930s and 1940s, are also quite specific solutions to city's climate. And the most important thing: such solutions are

still relevant today if you are willing to learn from existing structures.

It nevertheless remained necessary to install air conditioning at the Liebling Haus, didn't it?

Correct. Of course, today we have different ideas of comfort. Today, if you feel a draft in an old building, then you immediately write the landlord. Earlier, you would have just put on a jacket. And we noticed these different expectations in the Liebling Haus when you were sitting in a room discussing with ten or fifteen people. Air conditioning is necessary for anyone to be able to work at all. But we didn't want to just screw the units to the facade where they would be visible from the outside, as you unfortunately see so often with other structures. And then we found another possibility by looking at existing buildings: we accommodated the entire climate control technology in the cavities of the suspended balcony ceilings, where the balcony drainage is also routed. This keeps it hidden behind the wide concrete aprons that Dov Karmi had intended for shading. So we managed to avoid changing anything in how the building looks on the outside.

With your office, you supervised the entire building survey and then created guidelines for all the work that was to be done.

We had two tasks. The first was to act as consultants for the entire process; the second was the work on the facades—which was separated out from the rest of the process. At some point, it was decided to carry out the interior and exterior work independently, to speed things up. This also allowed the financing for each part to be organized separately, and we were able to start work on the facade while the plan for dealing with the interior spaces was still being discussed.

The facade plaster was originally to be completely removed, a practice that is quite common in Tel Aviv. A new plaster is then usually applied, which ideally looks similar to the old one. But that's when we said stop. Because if you sacrifice the plasterwork of the facade, a building loses so much of the patina it has acquired over the years, so much of its character. So we created a catalog of measures for conserving the plaster from the time when the building was constructed and for repairing the damaged areas. First, we were able to convince the German federal government, and then the Sto Foundation as well, to provide additional funds. The foundation was then also willing to not just bring in their own products, but to work with us in trying out new methods and materials, using pure mineral paints from Keimfarben applied as a kind of glaze after the restoration of the damaged plaster surfaces, thereby preserving the authenticity of the plaster. You always have to remember the importance of these details and the right materials, especially to make sure they remain compatible with the preserved remnants of the original. To put it in terms of heritage conservation: it's about material authenticity, and you have to take a critical look at the materials that the industry offers us today. The analysis this requires may be a bit more time-consuming, but it leads to more sustainable solutions where damage doesn't just occur after five years and everything has to be redone.

And was it possible to repair the plaster from when the building was constructed?

Yes. Now we have a facade at the Liebling Haus

in which as much material as possible from the original construction has been conserved, so that the traces of how the building has been used are also conserved. When you step close to the building, you can see these traces. But when I look at the building from a distance, it appears to be in its original state. This was something that was very important to us.

You said that the work on the facade was done separately from the work on the interior spaces. Does this mean that the conservation plans for the interior and exterior differ?
Not if you ask me. Both inside and out, it was a matter of conserving the different layers of time. The old windows were of such high quality that they could be repaired by apprentices from Berlin and Tel Aviv. It was also initially planned to partially replace the terrazzo floors, but then a decision was made to repair the existing ones. Repair and conservation are key concepts for the entire rebuild.

You describe the multilayered, unique solutions found for the Liebling Haus. Do you nevertheless see the project as a prototype for dealing with Tel Aviv's modernist heritage? Or is it rather an exceptional case, where there were options that would never be available in a "normal" renovation?
I would even say that this renovation can be applied to other projects in Tel Aviv. As far as I can see, the kind of renovations that are most common in Israel are where the old materials are taken out and everything is made new: new facades, new floors, new ceilings, new handrails. These are enormous interventions into the substance of the building. And it's not that these measures are adapted to fit the existing building; rather, concepts are just imposed on the structure. And I think that's the biggest insight to be had when you walk through the Liebling Haus today—that we did it the other way around. We looked at the possibilities offered by the existing building and then tailored our measures to meet them, right down to the details of the craftsmanship. It would be nice if more architects and building owners would take a close look at the structures they want to renovate and find solutions that conserves the unique qualities—the strengths and the intelligence—of the original building.

In my opinion, solutions are quite often possible that don't entail any serious sacrifice of comfort. Today, we have many technical possibilities for building in existing structures—but we have to actively ask for them; the industry doesn't offer them on its own. And beyond that, we need to relearn how to repair things. We need to move away from a disposable, new-build society back to a repair society, where the default is not to simply discard floors or windows but repair them. But to do this, you need to know how to do a good repair of these elements so that they then last for some time. Finding the right solutions requires imagination. But that's what's fun about dealing with an existing building. Repairing takes a lot more creativity than one generally expects.

Were there also places in the Liebling Haus that you couldn't renovate the way you wanted, that you perhaps prefer not to show today?
Honestly, there is no major intervention that I completely reject. I may be a little unhappy with the elevator and the emergency stairwell at the back. But these are elements that were absolutely necessary for the new use as an exhibition space, and that could not be ac-

commodated anywhere else in the residential building. In this respect, I think the solution at the back is basically correct. If anything, I would question the regulations and advocate that they be a little more relaxed when it comes to renovations of buildings like this. This is not a phenomenon exclusive to Israel but is true everywhere. The demands of fire protection, accessibility, or energy-efficient insulation can make the conversion of a wonderful building either impossible or considerably more difficult. Or they might result in a transformation that is hard to accept. Such conflicts can even apply to inconspicuous but important details such as the handrail in the stairwell. In the Liebling Haus, the handrail is interrupted at the landings, even though the regulations require handrails in public buildings to be continuous. So you end up arguing for a long time about a gap of a few centimeters, and you have to have the fortitude to keep having such tiring discussions. You have to become a kind of lawyer representing the building. However, the Liebling Haus has been a great stroke of luck overall, as everyone involved has mostly pulled together and many things became possible.

Do you already see evidence that the Liebling Haus renovation is spurring new ideas in discussions about heritage conservation in Israel?

That's something I can only speak to indirectly, through what Sharon tells me. She says that with all the tours and events at the building, there is a lot of interest in this type of renovation. My own experience at the opening was that many people from the neighborhood came and were very interested in how they could use this knowledge to renovate their own homes or apartments.

However, you always have to point out that what is at stake is not just the technical use value of a building, but an aesthetic, a kind of beauty that ties together the overall ensemble in Tel Aviv: the beauty that arises from the sum of the individual structures. My impression is that very many people in Tel Aviv are thinking only about their own building, not the overall context. You see that, too, in the additions you currently find all over the city, where the air rights over the buildings are sold like they are in New York, rather than respecting a holistic approach in protecting the small green spaces around the buildings, because you understand what the sum of these parts means for the climate in the whole city. Seeing these connections, the ways they are interwoven, is something Tel Aviv still needs to do.

In the end, the Liebling Haus is continuously evolving, constantly in search of its identity. To conclude our discussion: is there something you hope for in its future?

I think it's fantastic to see how people have already taken to the building. That's the real success of the project: that a lively, public site has been created with a café, garden, and exhibitions. And that the building can tell a story with its many visible layers of time. The most powerful thing, then, that the Liebling Haus can be is a permanent document that tells of its own renovation, in all of its complexity, with its debates and discussions and contradictions and histories of transfer: where did the materials come from, where did the people come from, what were their influences and ideas, and what is accordingly the foundation for the building's design? Making all of this something that can be permanently experienced, understood, touched, felt—that would be terrific.

"WE WANTED TO AVOID GIVING THE IMPRESSION THAT THE LIEBLING HAUS WAS A KIND OF ARCHITECTURAL-ARCHEOLOGICAL SPECIMEN, PRESERVED TO BE STUDIED."

From left:
Jörg Haspel (holding a recording device), Yossi Ribak, Daniella de Nur, Ingrid Haspel

Jörg Haspel, a German historic conservationist and state conservator in Berlin from 1995 to 2018, was a key advisor for the Liebling Haus renovation. In conversation with Florian Heilmeyer, he recalls his first impressions of the building and why he believes the unique strategies used in this renovation can be applied to other buildings.

How did you come to be part of the Liebling Haus project?

One starting point was probably the affinity we share with the modernist world heritage of the twentieth century. The Bauhaus buildings in Weimar and Dessau were inscribed on the UNESCO World Heritage List in 1996, as were Tel Aviv's White City in 2003 and six interwar modernist housing estates in Berlin in 2008. These inclusions drew a lot of attention, even beyond Germany and Israel, brightly signaling the opening up of UNESCO's World Heritage policy to architecture from the Modern Movement. That's what bonded us together, so to speak, especially since the issues in conservation and restoration that we face are similar—preserving new, often experimental building materials and constructions, dealing with standardized building elements, or the energy and building technology challenges posed by a contemporary retrofit.

By the way—relatively early on, in 2006, the German National Committee of the International Council on Monuments and Sites (ICOMOS) was among the initiators of a separate committee for the heritage of the twentieth century. In addition to the two Bauhaus cities of Weimar and Dessau, Tel Aviv and Berlin—with their modernist architectural heritage—played a key role from the very beginning. One could say that the label "Bauhaus" was what brought the otherwise quite different locations of Dessau, Weimar, and Berlin together with the "Bauhaus city" of Tel Aviv. For World Heritage Day 2013, for example, we worked with the Berlin Department for the Preservation of Historical Monuments to trace the route from Tel Aviv to the Schillerpromenade settlement in Berlin-Reinickendorf, also known as the White City. At that time, the first signs of the Israeli-German cooperation project Liebling Haus were already visible. And there was always the hope that the common heritage of architectural modernism might also serve to help establish a city partnership between Berlin and Tel Aviv.

When did you first visit the Liebling Haus and what was your impression?

I must have first encountered it during an ICOMOS lecture tour in the fall of 2014, though I only saw it from the outside. At the time, and this is still true today, there were two things I found remarkable. First, how historically well preserved the building was, as far as could be judged from the outside. In other words: there were no disruptive overhauls, no impairments from additions or extensions, no signs of ignorant modernizing interventions or incursions of new doors or windows, of insensitive repairs or immodest attempts at upgrading. Even the strip of garden greenery in front of the building, with the enclosure and pergola, had suffered but survived. In other words, what we had was the charming, typical case of a historic building that was starting to show its age and was a bit neglected, but for this very reason offered the highest degree of authenticity.

On the other hand, the urban environment seemed comparatively intact: the neighboring building blocks with their open development structure, the scale, the height of the buildings, the public spaces in the streets and squares ... The building had survived not as a singular exception in an inhomogeneous neighborhood, but as an integral part of a modern urban fabric. My first impression was later confirmed in the interior, as well, during the tours and meetings in the building. In short: the historical building needed no restorative interventions, but instead promised potential for a local strategy of conservation and public communication centered on existing architectural heritage.

What did this potential mean for the project of turning the Liebling Haus into an information and documentation center?
I believe that the condition of the building, as so historically well preserved, proved fascinating from the beginning and presented unique opportunities. The building's interior, too, was so clearly preserved and easy to grasp, from the structure of the floor plan to numerous historic features and some of the structural details. This included the largely undisturbed original entrance with the characteristic tiled staircase, the front doors to the apartments, and the interiors with their plastered wall and ceiling surfaces and floors, as well as the color finishes, stoneware tiles and terrazzo floors, fixtures and fittings, and period sockets and light switches. Countless discoveries and rediscoveries were also made through archival analysis and on-site archaeological research into the building, through information from historical witnesses, or through privately held documents left behind by individuals and families involved in the building's history.

Among the unexpected findings about the construction was evidence of building materials and furnishings that had come into the original construction of the Liebling Haus from Germany as part of the Haavara Transfer Agreement—including wall and floor tiles, sanitary ceramics from Villeroy & Boch, and modern door and window hardware including handles from the Wehag catalog. An example of the insight we gleaned from private documents and memories is the contribution from Daniella De-Nur, the Israeli co-chair of our Israeli-German advisory board, whose family lived on the second floor in the Liebling Haus over several decades and generations, and who was involved in building a trilingual website mylieblinghaus.com documenting the eventful history of the family and of how the Liebling Haus has been used.

You also mentioned the urban environment ...
Yes. This is precisely why the Liebling Haus is such an ideal location for a White City documentation center. If you take a walk around the area, you'll not only encounter an instruc-

tive spectrum of building types developed by owners and architects with the hopes of realizing a new Garden City in the spirit of classical modernism. You also find yourself spurred to make historical comparisons to pre- and early modernist contributions to the White City. You see this especially just a corner away from the Liebling Haus, on Bialik Square, where apartment buildings and the former city hall stand in a rather eclectic or late historicist architectural mode—precisely what Neues Bauen wanted to visibly distinguish itself from.

In renovating the Liebling Haus, we wanted to pursue and make visible two main programmatic aims. On the one hand, the building itself was to be preserved and made accessible as unchanged as possible, even in its structure, with its surfaces and the details of its construction. It was meant to be an architectural archive, a kind of collection of source material for architectural history. On the other hand, our intention was to practice the quasi-medical art of the most minimal intervention possible and to make sure visitors clearly see it. The conservation and renovation strategy was minimally invasive, if you will: it remained restricted to functionally mandatory adjustments, such as opening up the space where necessary to improve access or fire safety improvements, while avoiding time-consuming and costly technical retrofits.

From your point of view, what is special about the renovation and conservation of the Liebling Haus?

When it came to conserving the building as an archival source, we wanted to avoid giving the impression that the Liebling Haus was a kind of architectural-archeological specimen, preserved to be studied. By that I mean something like leaving visible excavations, cut-outs, or sequences of layers, or employing the stylistic device of showing the process by which traces were found and making demonstrative architectural interventions. Our strategy was to give as much information to visitors as possible while also maintaining as much of the building's historical authenticity and visual integrity as we could. This is what the Open for Renovation project was about—that is to say, the decision to have a visible construction site during the renovation, along with audiovisual materials about the building and its neighborhood presented in an app, including background information on the construction and history of use that is generally not accessible or known. I think the staircase is one of the most successful examples of subtle on-site communication about World Heritage you can find anywhere. Overall, then, what we didn't want was for the historic building to be an empty space for a cultural institution divided up into functions of visitor information, office, and archive, but rather a place of learning that itself functions as the object and messenger for the public outreach and communication program.

So do you see the Liebling Haus as a pilot project in Tel Aviv?

Certainly, the binational and especially the interdisciplinary approach, which went so far as to include the history of the building's use and of its residents, was extremely productive and promising. But it was also very complex and probably applicable to everyday practice only in exceptional cases. Of course, those involved hope that the project's basic approach to conservation and public communication about cultural heritage will prove to be transferable to other heritage construction sites, that it will set a precedent. That said, the renovation of this heritage building has meant almost entirely losing its original, primary use as an apartment building with private residential units, to instead create a public cultural institution. And that's one reason I don't want to overestimate its function as a multiplier, or at best I want to limit it to comparable cases where conservation means repurposing, where the residential function is lost, or to individual questions about renovations that aim to conserve a building.

When it comes to the issue of energy and air conditioning or the accessibility of residential buildings, the conversion of this heritage building can most likely offer a worthwhile contribution. The Liebling Haus could also provide inspiration for the practice of building surveys concerned with construction history and renovation, and for on-site presentations, provided that all stakeholders were to be offered a kind of publicly accessible *Schaudepot* for historic building materials and craftsmanship techniques. For both, however, it would be good to have a more systematic assessment of the measures taken in this project: What has proven to be effective, and in what ways? What do visitors to the building take away from the experience? How much of this comes from guided tours and events, and how much comes from the texts and audiovisual tools that have been included? What do visitors learn when they explore on their own? Perhaps it would be important to assess the experiences people have had since the building was opened in September 2019, with a focus on producing a representative self-evaluation and finding possible ways to optimize the site.

Which place, which room, which moment in the Liebling Haus do you find most successful or most impressive?

I'm not sure if the loggia-like balconies or the roof terrace of the building can be counted among its most impressive "spaces"—but I do know that many people, myself included, always especially enjoy spending time there. In fact, the building offers its visitors a number of very different opportunities to leave their homes and spend time outside, as it were, to experience the changing seasons and times of day. The balcony rooms with their windows or French doors also benefit in this sense, especially where they receive light from two sides across a corner.

I also find the rooms full of architectural discoveries, such as the kitchens or wet rooms with preserved or added fixtures or furnishings, to be continually inspiring. The traces from the demolition that have been left unfinished on the walls, ceilings, and floor are also striking, though not entirely successful. They mark voids and act as a reading guide for floor plan changes that were required by the quite recent conversion from apartment building to public visitor center. Or to say with the image of a minimally invasive art of medicine, I could have imagined employing forms of presentation that were gentler, more focused on healing, in the hopes of motivating visitors to emulate these practices in renovating their own homes in the White City. One thing, though, that always makes a welcome first and last impression on me is the entrance with the inviting goldfish tank.

What are your hopes for the Liebling Haus's future?

My hope is that the project will find a more stable form as an Israeli-German center for the preservation of modernist architecture, that it will be able to become established with long-term resources of its own, perhaps as a well-endowed foundation or association with powerful members who can offer solid backing. It might even be possible to continue international cooperation projects in the field of practical heritage conservation and craftsmanship, as we have seen successfully demonstrated to some extent in this renovation phase. In any case, the Liebling Haus and its team have the potential to become permanently established as an international hub in an international network of Bauhaus institutions, in Israel (together with the Bauhaus Center and Bauhaus Museum Tel Aviv) and in Germany (the Bauhaus Dessau Foundation, Bauhaus University Weimar, the Bauhaus Archive in Berlin). Likewise, I hope the Liebling Haus can become a focal point for multinational professional exchanges between institutions such as ICOMOS, DOCOMOMO, TICCIH, etc. One auspicious first signal in this direction might be if the Liebling Haus could once again welcome guests in the entryway with a water basin fulfilling its original function.

DETAILS

YAEL SCHMIDT

A German tile, stairwell, second floor

During the renovation work, a tile in the stairwell came loose (pp. 82 and 122), clearly marked on the back as a product of the German company Villeroy & Boch. How did this object get from the "Third Reich" to Tel Aviv in 1936? It was only through research to answer this question that the true scope of what was called the Transfer Agreement came to light: Jews fleeing Germany were not allowed to take cash but were instead forced to buy German products through Haavara, a Tel Aviv-based company, which they could then ship to Mandatory Palestine. This chance discovery in the stairwell led to the 2019 exhibition *Transferumbau* (Transfer Rebuild) at the Liebling Haus and at Bauhaus Dessau for the Bauhaus Centennial, sparking a wide-ranging discussion—first in Israel, then worldwide—about how these German products and building materials, acquired under duress, shaped the image of modernism in Tel Aviv.

Historical witnesses, stairwell, second floor

Which historical layers should be preserved during a renovation? The glass blocks in the stairwell were installed in the 1990s when some of the apartments were used as offices for the city administration. This was previously one of the entrance doors to the Asherman family's apartment. In a conventional renovation, these glass blocks would have likely been removed to restore the original design. For the renovation of the Liebling Haus, however, the history of the building's use has been preserved and made visible, including these blocks as historical witnesses with the same significance as all other elements of the structure.

Reading traces

Adapting a former residential building for the demands of a publicly accessible exhibition venue and neighborhood center unavoidably requires major interventions into the original structure. During the renovation of the Liebling Haus, the places where walls were removed were left visible and filled with new terrazzo cast. The history and changes made to the building thus become traces of the past and a visible narrative of what once was and what has happened here.

The ABCs of Terrazzo

The terrazzo workshop, part of Open for Renovation (p. 53), was led by Michael Dorrer from the Regensburg Terrazzo Studio.

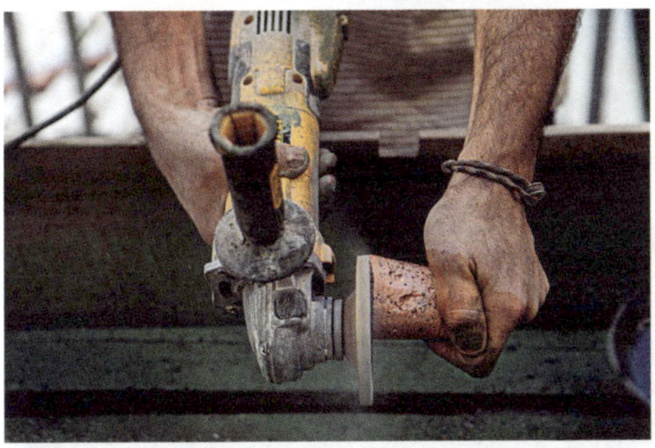

Cable trays, the café in the building today, first floor

Like the traces of the walls which were removed (p. 130) or the suspended ceilings over the balconies (p. 144), the exposed cable trays also reflect a compromise between preserving the original structure and meeting modern requirements. Should the new additions be concealed as much as possible? Or should the adaptations be left visible, creating a new layer of history that might change again in a few years?

Rounded corner, first floor

The curved reinforced concrete beam is an unusual detail, as rectangular shapes and grids are typically preferred for reinforced concrete structures. But Dov Karmi designed the Liebling Haus with two wings aligned to the boundaries of the lot, meeting at an angle of approximately 15 degrees. While this is hardly perceptible from the outside, the angle is practically celebrated inside the building with this dynamically curved detail. It's likely something that Dov Karmi and Zvi Barak were quite proud of.

Rounded corner, living room, third floor

The rounded corner in the Liebling Haus might strike an observer as a purely visual design element, echoing the dynamic curved building corners that were so popular in Mendelsohn's time—though we have no documented evidence that Dov Karmi was directly referencing Erich Mendelsohn. Regardless, the curvature of this wall plays a crucial role in the plan for natural ventilation. In the 1930s, technical devices for air conditioning were practically unknown. So like many other modern homes in Tel Aviv, the Liebling Haus relies on the natural principle of cross-ventilation: when windows are open, cool sea air flows into each apartment from the west and south and exits to the east, toward the garden. The rounded corner helps prevent air from stagnating where the walls meet. Understanding these building details is essential for any renovation.

Original features

Like many other buildings of its time, the Liebling Haus was designed down to every detail. Carelessly removing these features during renovation would change the overall composition. The Liebling Haus was fortunate in that many original elements were preserved, such as the mailboxes in the stairwell, or its door and window handles, light switches, and bathroom fixtures. Even the original windows with their wooden frames, precisely coordinated with the facade design, were not replaced but carefully restored and reinstalled in their original state.

A Window to Modernity

During this three-day workshop at the Liebling Haus, part of Open for Renovation (p. 53), participants learned methods for repairing windows and doors; the workshop was led by Robert Huber (zukunftsgeraeusche) from the Technical University of Berlin and master craftsman Frank Schultze.

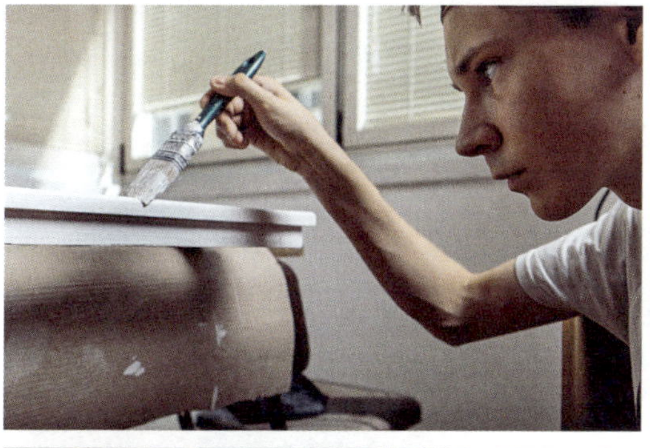

Modernism you can hold in your hand

The original fittings and handles on windows and doors—like the tiles in the stairwell (p. 128)—were also imports from a residential building under the Haavara Transfer Agreement. They were supplied by Wehag, Wilhelm Engstfeld AG, under license from S. A. Loevy—a Jewish family business from Berlin.

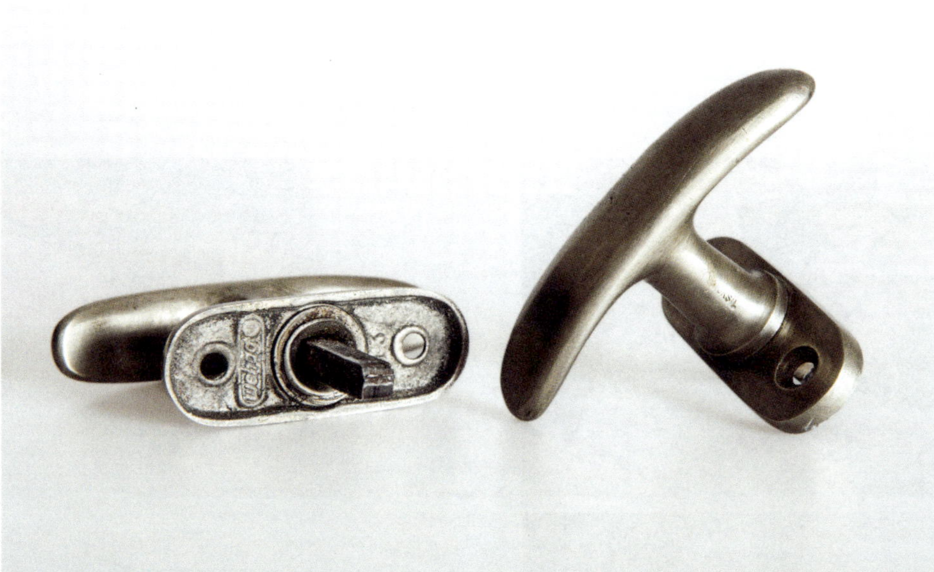

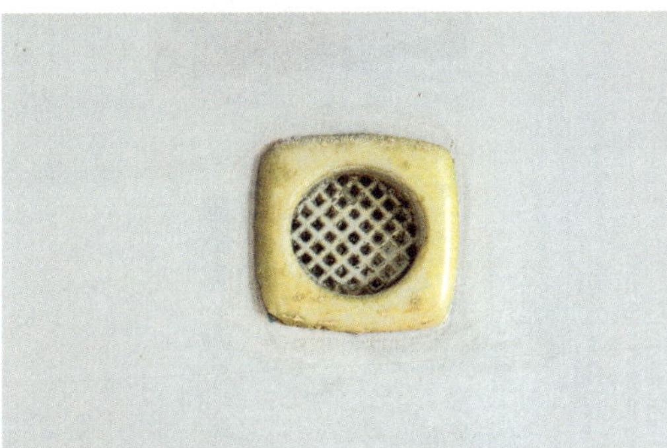

Strata and stories

This isn't damage, of course. Instead, the plaster layers at this corner have deliberately been left exposed, showcasing the wall construction all the way down to the pumice bricks. These bricks were most likely produced in Germany and brought to Tel Aviv under the Haavara Transfer Agreement (p. 81) with the "Third Reich." This element remains exposed at the top floor.

As found, bathroom, third floor
Many of the original components and fixtures in the Liebling Haus were preserved as they were found, including the bathroom on the third floor. One might wonder why this room was maintained in this condition. With its wear and tear, though, it tells a story not only of time's passage and the people who once lived here but also of entirely different ideas about comfort in 1930s Tel Aviv, when Tony and Max Liebling built a cutting-edge modern residence with the latest amenities.

Layers of paint, histories of color

During various painting workshops at the Liebling Haus, up to nine overlapping layers of paint were discovered, each telling a story of the building's changing uses and eras. For instance, we discovered that the palette of colors used at the Liebling Haus was based on the pastel colors used by Le Corbusier, rather than the color palette preferred by the Bauhaus.

Much More Than White

The painting workshop, part of Open for Renovation (p. 53), was led by architect Marlu Müller-Ortoff.

Hidden modernization, street-facing balconies, second and third floor

Every renovation requires compromises between meeting modern standards and preserving the original integrity of the building (see the interview with Winfried Brenne, pp. 114–119). Instead of mounting the new air conditioning units where they could be seen on the facade of the Liebling Haus—which would have disrupted Dov Karmi's carefully balanced facade design—the architects found an alternative solution. The high concrete skirts on the facade created unused space above the balconies. This space was originally closed with a suspended ceiling to prevent the hot air from being trapped in the concrete skirt. However, the space behind skirt and ceiling was empty, allowing the entire climate control system and new lighting to be installed here conveniently and invisibly. This setup maintained the original Bernoulli effect, naturally cooling the rooms inside.

Frankfurt kitchen, rear apartment, third floor

The traditional kitchen was a large room where people could eat, meet, and socialize. Modernism broke radically with this tradition, transforming the kitchen into a precisely measured functional space. No one took this concept further than Austrian architect Margarete Schütte-Lihotzky, with her 1926 design for the kitchens in Ernst May's public housing in Frankfurt am Main. The worldwide fame that Schütte-Lihotzky's Frankfurt Kitchen later achieved followed her for the rest of her life: "Had I known that this would be the one thing everyone would keep talking about, I would never have built that damn kitchen." She never intended her design to be a prototype. The kitchens first installed in the Liebling Haus were not exact reproductions of the Frankfurt Kitchens, but they were inspired by this design. The Frankfurt Kitchen shown in this image is an original, recently gifted to the Liebling Haus by the city of Frankfurt. It was slightly modified (p. 147) to fit the space, informed by archival documents on the building.

Air cupboard, kitchen, third floor
Despite all the modern amenities in the Liebling Haus, some things were still missing—among them, electric refrigerators. Instead, the apartments had an "air cupboard" like this one preserved in the former kitchen of the Scheuer family: a small shelf unit with a back made only of mesh and wooden slats. This design allowed relatively fresh air from the utility balcony to flow in and keep the food somewhat cool.

The Frankfurt Kitchen Migrates to Tel Aviv

This workshop, involving German carpentry apprentices and Israeli architecture students, was held under the auspices of the Berlin Max-Bill-Schule and Handwerkskammer Berlin as part of Open for Renovation (p. 53). It focused on analyzing, precisely reconstructing, and creating a digital model of the Frankfurt Kitchens in the Liebling Haus.

A culture of repair

The primary goal in renovating the Liebling Haus was to preserve as many of the original features and material as possible. The old terrazzo floors and the exterior and interior plaster, for example, were not completely stripped away; instead, the damaged areas were carefully repaired by hand (see the interview with Winfried Brenne, pp. 114–119)—a method that largely disappeared during the twentieth century in the industrialized construction industry and culture of quick disposal. Today, this approach needs to be thoroughly revived and relearned for the twenty-first century, incorporating new techniques, raw materials, and building materials.

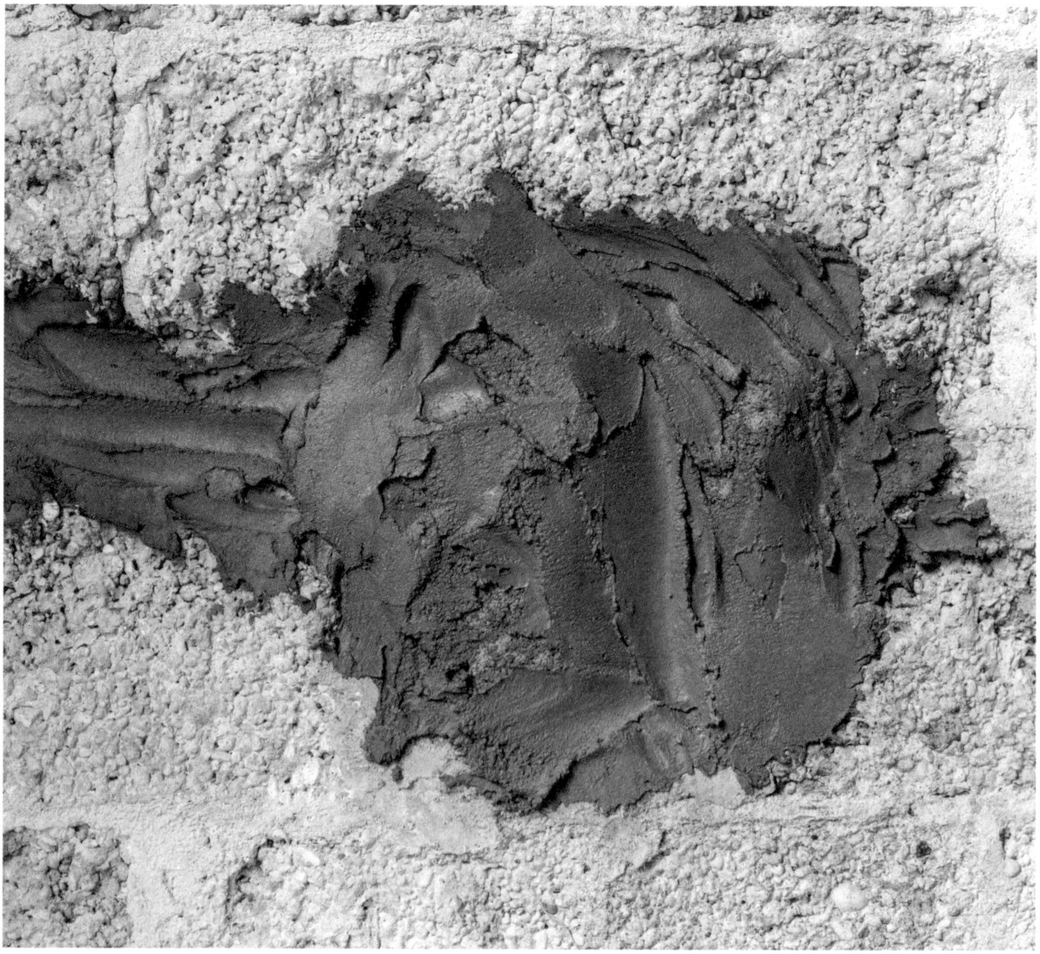

The Liebling Haus app offers audio recordings and texts providing additional information about these and many other details of the building.

THE

LIEBLING

HAUS

TOMORROW

What is to become of the Liebling Haus? What role can it—or must it, should it—play for the city of Tel Aviv? How can the building influence discussions about urban development and about how to deal with the heritage of modernism—in Tel Aviv and beyond? What experience does Tel Aviv have that gives it a head start over other cities? Can the way in which we are engaging with the Liebling Haus serve as a model for others? Can a cultural center be an activist for cultural change? And what do the many people who are involved in the building hope will lie in its future?

“THE LIEBLING HAUS HAS TO STAY A DYNAMIC PLACE. IT WILL NEVER BE FINISHED, NOR SHOULD IT BE.”

Sharon Golan ↑ and
Shira Levy Benyemini ↓

Together, **Shira Levy Benyemini** and **Sharon Golan** look to the future and, in conversation with Katrin Voermanek, formulate how they hope to see the Liebling Haus develop and consolidate its role as an activist institution with local and international impact.

How will the city change? And what does that mean for the Liebling Haus?

Sharon Golan: Tel Aviv is experiencing massive construction. This year alone, thousands of new apartments have been built, along with a new metro network with tunnels, light rail tracks, and stops. Experiencing the city like this is tremendously stressful. There are traffic jams every day, accompanied by the constant sound of bulldozers against an endless horizon full of yellow cranes. This is the reality of the city today. Tel Aviv can be something of a pilot project in this process of change for other metropolises that are also being forced to deal with climate change and crises. What we are witnessing here is the example of an adaptive city preparing to become a resilient place to live—no matter what the future holds.

Given these circumstances, the Liebling Haus needs to even more strongly assert the role of being a central hub for all of the issues related to living in the city. We want to make a difference. We want to be a platform, a think tank, and a place to share knowledge in ways that allow us to work together to better understand our built environment and continue to flexibly adapt to the ever-changing conditions in which we live.

Shira Levy Benyemini: I think the most important goal for the future is that we develop something like a *Liebling* way of thinking and speaking, which will then influence what is happening in the city. Maybe that sounds a bit pretentious, but I believe that many of the ideas we're working on now will really make a difference only a few years down the line: the return to Geddes and his Garden City, for example. That will end up influencing urban society, the authorities and the public—slowly, but I am sure of it. People will come to think differently about their city and its gardens. They'll stop using plastic everywhere, uprooting weeds hysterically, or asking about a new artificial turf for the playground their children use. They'll reflect on nature and the plants that grow in their city. I am sure that we can promote a new awareness for aesthetics, for sustainable renovation and for energy efficiency.

So in the future, if I have any question about architecture and the city, would I first want to go to the Liebling Haus?
SLB: I very much hope so, and not only in an archival sense. I think that we should develop into a central information site, one that also fosters research on new topics. And for that to happen, it's also necessary to expand our research activities and forms of outreach, and for that we haven't yet had enough budget or resources. I want the Liebling Haus to make an impact. If you need information, this should be the place to get it. I don't see it as a library, though, but as a collection of knowledge in the making. In the future, too, it will always be about exchange, about discourse. And this is also what helps to create civic engagement: this responsibility that each of us carries for the city, for society, for our young democracy.

If I see something going wrong, can I turn to the Liebling Haus? Is this a place where I can also find my inner activist?
SLB: That's what I would like to see. We have made some efforts in this direction, and this truly reflects who I am and is rooted in my past, the anchor from which I draw my inspiration. I want us to get involved. A project we did with creators from the Liebling program is a good example of this. When Zina Dizengoff Square was demolished, it certainly made a lot of people happy and improved the urban atmosphere and quality of the site for pedestrians. But we also heard voices from people who felt the way it used to be was important, for whom it felt familiar. So we thought of making some kind of souvenir, something very simple, with a simple design. We rescued small pieces from the demolition materials and distributed them to people who were interested. To our surprise, several thousand people wanted one of these mementos. We still get asked about it today. We have also participated in other protests, always together with other institutions, for example against an attempt to intervene into the exhibition at the Ramat Gan Museum of Israeli Art. There, a work of art was removed from an exhibition with the argument that it would offend the religious sensitivities of Orthodox Jews. Like many other institutions, we put up a black flag to show our opposition to this form of censorship. Even a decision to make exhibitions that deal with the problems of the public space, with destruction of buildings, with the Palestinian history of the Manshiya neighborhood, or with the design of urban spaces—this, too, is activism. Trying to make an impact, to build connections, and to initiate dialogue where none is taking place. Activism does not necessarily mean starting a riot. Rather, it means paying attention to others and making your voice heard. In this sense, our School of the City is a place where even children, that is to say, future generations, can learn what participation and activism mean—that it means taking responsibility for what matters to you.

Given all these indications of what is coming, does the Liebling Haus have to change, too?
SLB: To do this, the Liebling Haus doesn't necessarily need to grow qualitatively as an institution. It should maintain its relevance and find a way to go deeper and not be a part of a superficial discourse. This would be possible only if a dynamic and adaptive approach is kept as much as possible, in terms of both the content and the physical space. The one thing we really could use is an archive to collect

With a view of the constantly growing skyline of Tel Aviv, the Liebling Haus serves as a place to think about the city's possible future. What could Tel Aviv become? Could it once again be the Garden City originally proposed in Patrick Geddes's plan, but adapted to the changes the city has seen (p. 74)?

building elements that, until now, have been carelessly thrown away here during renovations. The spaces in the building are constantly changing anyway, just like we do as people. They are influenced not only by our changing programs, but also by the visitors. It was important for us not to "freeze" the spaces in any one state. The Liebling Haus is itself a dynamic and constantly evolving place. It will never be finished, nor should it be.

Is there anything missing from the program? What specific topics or formats ought to be added in the future?
SG: We want to provide more support for thought leaders. One way we are doing this, for example, is by developing the program A Field Trip to Urban Futures: A Bilateral Action Research Project of Thought Leadership with the Negev School of Architecture and the Hochschule für bildende Künste Hamburg. We are focusing on the climate crisis and the environmental and social tensions it is exacerbating, particularly in heterogeneous societies. Our view is that the situation in Israel can serve as a concrete example of what the future holds for other Western countries: growing conflicts between progressive and traditionalist forces and various religious groups, leading to the erosion of democratic values and social cohesion. Turning to a new kind of collaboration among researchers from different disciplines, we are working to find mechanisms for dealing with such conflicts, both technologically and culturally.

So the Liebling Haus doesn't want to be a white villa in the White City that we visit with devotion, but a person you can talk to, ask for advice, who makes their voice heard and has an influence throughout the city and far beyond. Is that right?
SLB: Absolutely. And we don't want to just wait for those who come here on their own. We want to actively increase the intensity of connections with other institutions and thus our outward influence. We want to go out into our neighborhood. We are part of the city government and want to be seen and heard there, as well. We want to network more with other community centers across the country and internationally, and to exhibit and share our work and ideas there. That's my plan for the future.

SG: The Liebling Haus will continue to be the right place for understanding, acknowledging, and addressing the complex challenges of tomorrow. All imaginable polarities collide here in one point, but we can bridge the gap between them—between traditional craftsmanship and cutting-edge new technologies, between political decision-makers and those active on the ground, and not least between Israel and Germany.

In 2022, French artist Laure Catugier projected her stop-motion video *Blitz: Architecture Is Frozen Music #8* on the facade of the Liebling Haus. Catugier produced this work during her residency at the Liebling Haus. The curator was architect Sabrina Cegla.

VOICES

"My wish for the Liebling Haus is that it continue to feel a connection to the triad of history, the present, and the future: that it commemorate its construction and its builders, preserve the building itself through close-knit Israeli-German cooperation, and inspire the youth of both countries to carry on this torch."

Gunther Adler is a founding father of the Liebling project and was chairman of the board of trustees. From 2014 to 2018, he was a state secretary in the civil service—the highest possible rank—at the German Federal Ministry for the Environment, Nature Conservation, Building and Nuclear Safety and then at the Federal Ministry of the Interior for Building and Homeland Affairs until February 2019. From 1 March 2019, he was managing director of personnel at Autobahn GmbH of the Federal Republic of Germany. Since January 2024, he has been deputy managing director of the German Property Federation (ZIA) in Berlin.

"I hope that the Liebling Haus will continue to solidify its reputation as a distinctive and welcoming cultural space. A hidden architectural gem tucked away amid the city, it raises awareness toward urbanism and modernism through art exhibitions, international residency programs, research, and educational activities. I dare pray that it will receive the financial support it needs for its programs, and for the center to continue influencing and touching the minds and hearts of the citizens of Israel and the residents of Tel Aviv-Yafo."

Revital Ben-Asher Peretz is a curator based in Tel Aviv-Yafo, an art consultant to the mayor of Tel Aviv-Yafo, and a member of the executive board of the Liebling Haus.

"I see Liebling Haus as a dynamic space, reflecting diverse attitudes, practices, and perspectives on the built environment and its heritage; as a space for learning which encourages a broad discourse and an open exchange of ideas, while facilitating critical inquiry and action. I wish it to continue developing as a platform for disrupting narratives and imagining possible futures; a space for rethinking architecture and the architect's role amidst pressing local and global challenges."

Sabrina Cegla is an Israeli-German architect and curator. As founding member of Liebling Haus (since 2015), she has contributed to articulating its vision and values. She has initiated and curated numerous projects, including the permanent exhibition and the Open for Renovation educational building site. Today, she is the senior curator of exhibitions of the Liebling Haus and directs its residency program. Cegla holds a bachelor's degree in architecture and a master's degree in history and theory of architecture from Tel Aviv University.

"I wish for Liebling what we all wished at the beginning ... I still hope it will be the beating heart of a comprehensive archive for all Bauhaus buildings and projects around Israel. A lighthouse for current professional architects who are seeking information and wish to deepen their knowledge of the era and technical characteristics of Bauhaus and modernism. Now, in its fifth year having gone thorough meticulous renovation and opening as the Liebling Haus, it is time to develop into an inspiring research and study foundation."

Daniella De-Nur, owner and Chief Editor of Daniella De-Nur Publishers and former co-chair of the Liebling Haus Advisory Committee together with Prof. Jörg Haspel. Her connection to the Liebling Haus is personal, as she is a direct descendant of the Ashermans who lived on its second floor from 1937 until 1965. Daniella lived with her grandparents at the Liebling Haus from 1952 until 1965. Please find more information on: www.mylieblinghaus.com

"I hope that the Liebling Haus will be an example of a building that preserves its unique cultural heritage, even when it absorbs new interpretations and functions. The practice of conservation is embodied in the small details, where the hand of the architect is felt and where the rich history of the building is also revealed in its material form. The activities of conservation are interpretive, personal, and above all unassuming."

Rivka Karmi is an architect continuing the office of Arch. Ram Karmi, Dov Karmi's son, the original architect of the Liebling Haus. Rivka graduated from the Faculty of Architecture and Urban Planning at the Technion Haifa in 1984 and earned a master's degree in gender studies from Lesley College in 2001. Besides running her own office, Rivka is also a teaching fellow at the Azrieli School of Architecture at Tel Aviv University.

"Heavens, Liebling! My darling! Happiest congratulations on your eighty-eighth birthday! Please keep surprising us with lightning-smart exhibitions, lively workshops, craft seminars, and great events. Stay bold, free, and wild. Let us grow with you, as we did with Open for Renovation. Let us live, grasp, hear, see, feel, smell, and taste our history. Stay open to communication, inspiration, illusion, and encouragement that speaks for itself. Take care, Liebling!"

Ellen Kugler has directed the team responsible for White City Tel Aviv at the Rhineland-Palatinate Office for Federal Construction since the project began. She studied politics, history, and geography and has worked as an editor and journalist.

"I wish for Liebling Haus to continue its development and become a bilateral center that will enhance the multicultural dialogue between Germany and Israel. That it draw young generations from all over the world to learn about the importance of architecture and design for our lives. And that it serve as a cultural center emphasizing creativity and innovation in the heart of Tel Aviv."

Nili Lamdan has been director of resource development at the Tel Aviv Foundation since 2011 and served as a member of the Liebling Haus board of trustees until December 2023.

"I hope Liebling Haus will become a center for researchers looking for ways to upgrade the principles of the Modern Movement for a new way of living, as expressed in the White City; architects sharing knowledge online and through monthly gatherings; teenagers eager to explore the White City and its architecture; and children taking their first steps in exploring buildings."

Nitza Metzger-Szmuk is an architect and professor of architecture. She was the founder of the conservation team at the municipality of Tel Aviv in 1990 and author of the nomination file for Tel Aviv to be included in the UNESCO World Heritage list in 2002. She is owner of Nitza Szmuk Architects, a practice which focuses on conservation and new ways of inhabiting the White City.

"I envision Liebling Haus as a constantly changing beacon in the White City of Tel Aviv, igniting curiosity and innovative design in all things urban. Celebrating the past, fostering partnerships, focusing on our cities' residents—these things will position Liebling Haus as a research hub, blazing new paths in urban planning, strengthening our shared public spaces, around the globe."

Hila Oren, CEO of the Tel Aviv Foundation, is a city maker and a passionate urbanist, with vast experience in city branding and marketing. She is a world-renowned expert, speaker, and educator on smart cities and on reducing the loneliness pandemic via the development of public space.

"Liebling Haus allows people like me, who create in photography, to observe a changing space that aims to suspend time, just like the act of photography itself—to stop time in order to convey a feeling, change, an idea. The spaces in the building and their changing contents allow me to detach and observe, turning them into single images, while also feeling and understanding more broadly how the city is changing around me over time. I hope that this special place will continue to allow this lingering—an experience that has scarcely survived in the bustle of life outside."

Yael Schmidt is a photographer in Tel Aviv. She has been documenting the Liebling Haus since 2017, interlacing the Haus and the city in a variety of projects. She is also the author of the photo essays in this book.

"My hope is that the Liebling Haus will remain an inspiring place of exchange and a functioning meeting place for the neighborhood, and that it will continue to be living testimony to the historical and architectural significance of the White City for Germany and Israel."

Guido Spars is a German urban and real estate economist and university professor. He has been the founding director of the German Federal Bauakademie Foundation since March 2021. He is a member of the Liebling Haus board of trustees.

"My hope is that the Liebling Haus will continue to serve as a site for international encounters that foster intergenerational exchange between science and crafts, and between cultures and individuals, and that it will remain a place of peace. The Sto Foundation is proud to have helped make this jewel in the White City sparkle on an international stage by supporting craftwork projects in 2019 with twenty-three young plasterers and painters. Since then, the participants from Germany have left a little piece of their heart in Israel."

Till Stahlbusch is chair of the Sto Foundation board. By providing a grant of 80,000 euros in 2019, the foundation made it possible to send young craftspersons and master craftspersons to the site and thus to renovate the facade of the Liebling Haus in line with the conservation requirements for a heritage building.

"I see the Liebling Haus continuing to be a place of exchange about architecture and society—in the broadest sense: How do we adapt our building in the face of the climate crisis? What can we learn for the future from autochthonous architecture in the Levant and from modernist architecture?

The Liebling Haus is the place to convince Tel Aviv residents that, despite the enormous need for housing in Tel Aviv, the buildings of the White City are very valuable and should be protected—not only the facades, but also structural details such as thermometer windows or natural ventilation options. I hope that this important discourse will continue to find its place in the Liebling Haus in the future."

Regina Stephan is an art and architectural historian. Since 2008 she has been a professor for the history of architecture and urban development at Hochschule Mainz, University of Applied Sciences. From 2013 to 2019 she was a member of the advisory board, where she became closely involved with the foundation of the White City Center/Liebling Haus.

"My wish for the future of the Liebling Haus is not only that it remain an important cultural institution within the White City, but also that it develop into an advisory center for renters and property owners who are interested in restoring and preserving these historical buildings. For me, establishing the Liebling Haus and professionally restoring the building was an incredibly meaningful project. I hope the Liebling team will be able to continue their professional work and enjoy great success, and that they will always have the courage to make the right decisions."

Christoph Strohschneider is an architect and the former director of the Rhineland-Palatinate Office for Federal Construction, which hosts the team responsible for the White City Tel Aviv project. From the summer of 2016 until his departure from the office at the end of 2019, he played an important role in the bilateral Liebling Haus project as an advisor and pacesetter—a true rock in the storm who was appreciated especially for speaking openly and directly.

"Dear Liebling Haus, you have become a fantastic center for information, inspiration, discussion, and new conversations. I hope that you will remain attractive as a vibrant site not only for experts, but for everyone who lives here and comes to visit. You are a wonderful place for gathering and meeting new people, and you offer tremendous opportunities for personal exchanges between Germany and Israel. Build on these strengths, and you'll be doing a lot of things right."

Matthias Vollmer is an undersecretary and head of Department B I 6 (Sponsorship and Construction for Foreign Armed Forces) at the German Federal Ministry of Housing, Urban Development and Building. After studying architecture, he initially worked at the Federal Office for Building and Regional Planning beginning in 1997, moving to the Federal Ministry of Transport, Building, and Housing in 2002. He has been supporting the White City Tel Aviv project since 2012.

"Like any well-crafted piece of architecture, the Liebling Haus is an inspiring, contemporary, and welcoming place for all, and part of the cultural heritage of Tel Aviv-Yafo. It's a cultural hub and a key component of Bialik Square, with its surrounding multidisciplinary network of museums. I envision it evolving, through the center's vision as a house of architecture, into a place that fosters discussion and research for both experts and the general public, acting as a bridge between art, design, and architecture, interwoven with the daily cultural life of the ever-evolving city."

Giyora Yahalom is a screenwriter, dramaturge, and television content creator. He is currently the head of the Department of Culture and Arts at the municipality of Tel Aviv-Yafo.

... AND THE DAY AFTER TOMORROW!

In the end, after all the texts and images, the things that should become more meaningful are the experiences one has when visiting a building whose vision essentially unites everything one can know and learn about a city—that's when city, building, and garden converge to become a microcosm of the urban experience.

Since we first stepped into the Liebling Haus, before its opening as a cultural center, we have sought to create a center in the building that retains a sense of intimacy, as a center with an inward, calm focus. And yet we also want to feel the city, as a space where things are happening, in the way they do on city streets and squares. While we see the walls as layers of time that will remain long after we are gone, we also realized that the building itself will continue to take in everything that is happening in the city, on all of its levels, far into the future. The residential space that has gradually developed into a public center invites relationships and encounters, similar to the waypoints that exist in the urban fabric. Since its opening, the building has adapted to the public mission with which it has been entrusted. The generous spaces have welcomed the new tenants and users with gentle curiosity. As with any public space or city, the building thus finds a new identity in the spirit of its users.

While the foundations of the city tell of the layer of the White City, so too does the building that has stood for nearly a century. But like the changing city and the comings and goings of its residents, the building also responds to ecological and social shifts. In the practice of architecture and urban planning, we always strive to sensitize the building, which has become a center of knowledge over time, to the needs of the environment. Just as urban planning—at least in a city that means well by its users—presupposes the conservation of aesthetic and human values, supported by listening, sensitivity to the environment, and vigilance toward changing needs, the center should function in ways that are relevant to how it is used by the various groups of people who come to know it—city residents, visitors, and professionals.

The work in research and education done in the center enhances its artistic and public work through listening, conversations, and learning, helping to realize processes situated at the intersection of planning institutions, the city administration, and the community.

The idea that the city's first ideas were brought on the waves of the sea to settle in Tel Aviv continues to find new expression today. And yet this building is also rooted in the city, in the history of this place and the material of its construction, just as it manages to respond to changes in the city, to play with them in concert.

The collaboration with the German federal government allows us to keep to our vision for the Liebling Haus—as a place that preserves and revitalizes the architecture of modernism and the White City, and that serves as a point of contact for the urban community in Tel Aviv. We want this to be a center that strives for excellence in the fields of research, professional training, and knowledge in the area of heritage conservation and architecture.

In the coming years, we will work to give the center a leading role as a site for exchanging ideas and fostering discourse for the community of those concerned with heritage conservation and urban development. We will convey the physical, theoretical, cultural, and social aspects of heritage conservation and of the city, and engage in dialogue with the public through cultural and artistic activities. In the coming years, our aim is to establish the center as a platform to proactively, and meaningfully, advance topics in research, architecture, and urban planning. Since urban issues are a challenge for cities in both Israel and Germany, our efforts are intended to enable bilateral relations and the exchange of knowledge between these two countries.

Shira Levy Benyemini

AUTHORS

Sören Bartol holds a degree in political science and has been a member of the German Bundestag since 2002; the parliamentary state secretary to the German federal minister for Housing, Urban Development, and Construction since December 2021; and federal commissioner for the German-Greek Assembly (DGV) since 2023. From 2013 to 2021, he served as deputy chairman of the SPD parliamentary group in the Bundestag, overseeing the areas of construction, housing, urban development, and municipalities; digital agenda, transport and digital infrastructure; and (from 2018) the economy. Since 10 January 2023, Bartol has been co-chair of the Liebling Haus board of trustees.

Winfried Brenne is an architect, technical draftsman, and mechanical designer. He studied architecture in Wuppertal and Berlin, where he founded a joint office with Helge Pitz in 1977 that he has continued in partnership with Franz Jaschke since 1990, and with his son Fabian since 2018. The office has not only carried out the historic preservation of modernist icons—such as the Bauhaus Building by Walter Gropius in Dessau, the Academy of Arts by Werner Düttmann in Berlin, or the former ADGB Trade Union School by Hannes Meyer in Bernau—but has also restored, in accordance with historic preservation standards, the six Berlin Modernist Housing Estates recognized as UNESCO World Heritage Sites, as well as museums, residential buildings, theaters, and historic estates from all eras. Brenne has held memberships with the Deutscher Werkbund since 1993, the Akademie der Künste, and the German National Committee of ICOMOS since 2000. At the Liebling Haus, he and his office took on responsibility in 2014 for the building survey and site analysis, from which he developed a comprehensive catalog for all restoration measures. His office directly handled the careful restoration of the facade.

Udi Carmely is the city engineer for the municipality of Tel Aviv-Yafo. Carmely holds a bachelor's degree in architecture from Tel Aviv University and a master's degree in urban planning from the Technion in Haifa. He has been involved in the fields of planning and construction, including in the field of urban renewal, for approximately twenty years, and he has held several management positions in the engineering directorate of the municipality of Tel Aviv-Yafo, outlining and leading many projects in the fields of housing, urban renewal, transportation, and more. Since 2018 he serves as a co-chair of the board of trustees for the Liebling Haus.

Sabrina Cegla is an architect and curator. She is the senior curator at the Liebling Haus and has been part of its founding team since 2015, coformulating its vision and values. Cegla has initiated and curated many events, platforms, exhibitions, and projects at the Liebling Haus, including the permanent exhibition *Exceptional: The White City—An Everyday Heritage*; the educational construction site project Open for Renovation; and the residency program HaDira (The Apartment). In her curatorial practice she foregrounds multidisciplinary, critical investigations of the built environment, architectural practices, and heritage in light of local and planetary challenges. Cegla holds a bachelor's degree in architecture and a master's degree in history and theory of architecture from Tel Aviv University. In addition, she has taught critical conservation at Shenkar College of Engineering, Design and Art, and has founded an independent architecture and design studio specializing in exhibition and interior design for projects in the fields of education and hospitality.

Sharon Golan is an architect specializing in the field of conservation, urbanism, and sustainability. She holds a bachelor's degree in architecture from IIT Chicago, a master's degree from TU Berlin, and a second master's degree in conservation and urban planning from the Technion in Haifa. During her work as a conservation architect in the municipality of Tel Aviv-Yafo, she laid the foundation for the creation of the Liebling Haus by connecting Tel Aviv and Germany's joint interest in the shared heritage of the Bauhaus. In her current role as head of the research lab at Liebling Haus, she aims to connect theory and academia with the practice of urban planning, while promoting contemporary bilateral Israeli-German projects focusing on sustainable holistic initiatives in the field of conservation, retrofitting, and urban planning.

Jörg Haspel graduated in 1981 with two degrees, one in architecture and urban planning in Stuttgart and another in art history and cultural studies in Tübingen. Haspel then became a custodian in the Monument Protection Authority of Hamburg and taught at Hamburg University. From 1992 to 2018, he served as the Berlin state curator of historic monuments (Landeskonservator), and from 2012 to 2021 as president of ICOMOS Germany. Since 2014, he has chaired the board of trustees of the German Foundation for Monument Protection (Deutsche Stiftung Denkmalschutz). He is a permanent member of the Expert Group on Urban Heritage Conservation of the federal government in Germany and a founding member of the International Scientific ICOMOS Committee on Twentieth-Century Heritage Preservation (ISC 20C). He has been continuously involved with the Liebling Haus project as an expert advisor.

Florian Heilmeyer is a freelance journalist, editor, author, and curator. Since his studies in architecture in Berlin and Rotterdam, he has been involved in many international publication and exhibition projects, including the German contributions to the Architecture Biennale in 2008 and 2012, and most recently in the editorial team for the federal research project *Planen und Bauen im Nationalsozialismus* (Planning and Architecture under National Socialism). He regularly publishes essays and critiques in a wide range of international print and online media. He lives in Berlin and Oberammergau.

Jeremie Hoffmann is an architect and historian (PhD). Since 2005, he has been head of the conservation department of Tel Aviv-Yafo. Hoffmann has taught architecture history and theory of the Modern Movement at various universities; he currently teaches at Negev School of Architecture in Be'er Sheva. He has written a number of books on the architectural heritage and history of Tel Aviv, including *Aforia: Architecture of Independence 1948–1977* and *PoMo: An Architecture of Privatization 1977–2003*. He is one of the founders of the Liebling Haus and an advisor to its management team.

Ellen Kugler is a journalist, presenter, and since 2016, the head of the White City Tel Aviv office at the German Federal Office for Building and Regional Planning in Rhineland-Palatinate. She studied political science, history, and geography in Bonn, Frankfurt, and Aberystwyth (Wales). Since her first stay in Tel Aviv, she has known that "In Israel, you have to believe in miracles to be a realist."

Shira Levy Benyemini is a city planner, urban designer, and curator, with expertise in urban regeneration processes, community planning, and conservation, who explores the interconnections of urban transformation, particularly involving cultural and artistic activities. She is the founding CEO and artistic director of Liebling Haus. Today she teaches at the Negev Architecture School in Beer Sheva and instructs creators and scholars in developing scholarly and artistic urban activities as a part of the residency programs in Liebling Haus.

Yael Schmidt is a photographer who lives and works in Tel Aviv. She is a graduate of the MA fine art program at Central Saint Martins, University of the Arts, London (2005), and the photography program at Hadassah College, Jerusalem (1999). Her creative work has been exhibited internationally, most recently at TEO Museum, Herzliya in 2022. Since the Liebling Haus was founded in 2017, she has been documenting it with a variety of projects that interlace the Haus and the city.

Katrin Voermanek works as a freelance writer, consultant, and university instructor in Berlin. After studying architecture and urban planning at the University of Stuttgart, she served as an editor at the *BauNetz Online-Dienst*, since then regularly publishing in magazines, newspapers, and books. She advises architects on communication issues and teaches on the topic of "language as a design tool" at institutions including the TU Berlin, BTU Cottbus, and Berlin International University of Applied Sciences. Her book *Typisch Posener* about the architecture critic Julius Posener was published in 2019 by JOVIS Verlag.

Present members of the board of trustees
Sören Bartol, parliamentary state secretary, German Federal Building Ministry; co-chair
Revital Ben-Asher Peretz, curator, art consultant to the mayor of Tel Aviv-Yafo
Udi Carmely, architect, head of the City Engineering Administration, Municipality of Tel Aviv-Yafo, co-chair
Erez Ella, architect, founding partner, principal architect, HQ Architects, faculty member at the Bezalel School of Architecture, head of Research Unit
Dr. Herlind Gundelach, state minister in Hamburg (retired)
Susanne Haus, president of the Frankfurt-Rhein-Main Chamber of Crafts
Dr. Hila Oren, chief executive officer at the Tel Aviv Foundation
Prof. Dr. Guido Spars, founding director of the Federal Bauakademie Foundation, Berlin

Former members of the board of trustees
Gunther Adler, German federal state secretary
Dr. Sigrid Bias-Engels, former team leader in the office of the German federal government commissioner for culture and the media
Dr. Andreas Eberhardt, former chief executive officer at the Foundation German-Israeli Future Forum
Orly Erel, director of the Urban Planning Department, Municipality of Tel Aviv-Yafo
Ronit Ferber, head of the Community Administration, Municipality of Tel Aviv-Yafo
Oded Gvuli, architect, former head of the City Engineering Administration, Municipality of Tel Aviv-Yafo
Nili Lamdan, Tel Aviv Foundation
Dafna Lev, former director of the Education Administration, Municipality of Tel Aviv-Yafo
Julia Rust von Krosigk, former deputy director of the Federal Bauakademie Foundation, Berlin
Volkmar Vogel, German parliamentary state secretary; co-chair
Marco Wanderwitz, German parliamentary state secretary; co-chair

Advisory board (until 2019)
Winfried Brenne, Winfried Brenne Architekten, Berlin
Daniella De-Nur, publisher, former resident of the Liebling Haus; Israeli co-chair of the advisory board
Prof. Zvi Efrat, Bezalel Academy of Arts and Design, Jerusalem
Candida Gertler, Outset Contemporary Art Fund
Prof. Dr. phil. Dipl.-Ing. Jörg Haspel, former state curator (Landeskonservator) and director of the Berlin State Conservation Authority (Landesdenkmalamt Berlin); German co-chair of the advisory board
Dr. Annemarie Jaeggi, director of the Bauhaus-Archiv / Museum für Gestaltung
Prof. Nitza Metzger-Szmuk, conservation architect, former head of the Conservation Department, Israel Institute of Technology (Technion Haifa)
Dr. Claudia Perren, former director of the Bauhaus Dessau Foundation
Prof. Regina Stephan, University of Applied Sciences Mainz
Petra Wesseler, president of the German Federal Office for Building and Regional Planning (BBR)
Meira Yagid, curator of design and architecture at Tel Aviv Museum of Art
Nava Zukerman, artistic director of Tmu-na Theater

Staff from German federal ministries and related agencies
Thomas Biermann, consultant to Parliamentary State Secretary Vogel
Rebekka Boos, architect, Agency for Federal Construction Rhineland-Palatinate on behalf of the German ministry
Klara Geywitz, German federal building minister
Dr. Matthias Hackstein, consultant to State Secretary Adler
Clemens Haury, architect, technical director
Miriam Hohfeld, policy officer
Nicole Ludwig, architect, technical director
Michael Marten, consultant to State Secretary Adler
Ralf Poss, former subdepartment head, ministerial director
Ulrike Probst (former Office White City Project, Magdeburg)
Andreas Raible, consultant to Parliamentary State Secretary Wanderwitz
Ulrike Rose, project advisor, cultural manager on behalf of German federal officials
Lucas Rosenthal, consultant to Parliamentary State Secretary Bartol
Christoph Strohschneider, architect, former director, Agency for Federal Construction Rhineland-Palatinate on behalf of German federal officials
Matthias Vollmer, architect, division head

Warmest thanks to
Ing. Shlomi Dagan, project manager on behalf of the Tel Aviv Foundation

... the planning team
Ada Karmi-Melamede, architect
Rivka Karmi, architect
Dan Hasson, architect
Jonathan Cohen, architect
Winfried Brenne, architect

... the construction team
Arco Group
Keimfarben
Sto Foundation
Knobelsdorff-Schule, Berlin
Max-Bill-Schule, Berlin
Susanne Boy, Chamber of Crafts, Berlin
Robert Huber, zukunftsgeraeusche, Berlin
Dipl.-Min. Dr. Norbert Hoepfer, geologist
Marlu Müller-Ortloff, architect
Adi Reich

... the best team ever
Sabrina Cegla
Anat Levy
Moran Novan
Yael Schmidt
Dalit Simhoni-Bar
Miki Simone
Anat Ran
Carmel Sela
Ran Malul
Sara Kaufman
Liav Levy

Michal Lichtenstein
Tamar Goldstein
Tomer Unger
Avigail Paiten
Anat Groysmann
Melina Hartmann
Dr. Catherine Rochant
Tsuf Bar On

... together with the team
from the School of the City
Director and curator:
Eran Eizenhamer
Producer: Maya Kremer

Guides, writers, and
participants (2017–24):
Daniel Oksenberg
Tal Alperstein
Tamara Anna Efrat
Roni Binder
Shai Ben-Ari
Naama Bar-Or
Anat Barzilai
Ayelet Gazit
Michal David
Oree Holban
Elad Horn
Or Herz
Oded Webman
Ana Wild
Rotem Volk
Yoav Weinfeld
Haim Hakimyan
Shira Tabachnik
Rany Sarah Yiftach
Gil Harabagio Cohen
Shahaf Levy
Ruth Leonov
Hila Cohen-Schneiderman
Maayan Mozes
Dana Mor
Lou Moria
Shir Moran
Razia Mizrahi
Yuli Maroz
Kineret Haya Max
Michal Svironi
Dganit Senesh
Roy Fabian
Merav Kamel
Roni Raviv
Yoni Raz Portugali
Omer Shach
Noa Simhayof Shahaf
Ishai Shapira Kalter
Hilit Shefer
Gai Sherf

Café Lev:
Itamar Weiner
Nurit Egozi
Dana Yankelevitch

... to all the wonderful people who inspired us over the years
Yarden Goz
Nova Dobel
Moran Shambar
Gaya Davidson
Klod Aviram
Vered Salem
Noa Hollander
Liya Kochavi
Hadas Zemer Ben Ari
Antje Eiger
Milana Gitzin-Adiram

The Liebling Haus team, 2024

Yarden Diskin
Dr. Marianne Zepp
Michael Gordon
Shula Widrich
Noam Noy
Efrat Goldmann
Hila Cohen-Schneiderman
Rachel Gottesman
Ilit Azoulay
Lou Moria
Nir Shauloff
Jonathan Touitou
Racheli Kinrot
Oded Kutok
Yanek Iontef
Tom Darom
Ran Tal
Nirit Nelson
Shay Zilberman
Irit Tamari
Claude Aviram
Ohad Kabri

Special thanks go to the first supporters who made this project come to life when we were still dreaming about it
Dr. Jeremie Hoffmann, architect, head of the Conservation Department, Municipality of Tel Aviv-Yafo
Reinhold Robbe, former president of the Israeli German Society, Berlin
Steffen Claudio Lemme, former member of the German Bundestag
Winfried Brenne, architect, conservation architect of the Liebling Haus and member of the advisory board
Prof. Dr. phil. Dipl.-Ing. Jörg Haspel, former state curator (Landeskonservator) and director of the Berlin State Conservation Authority (Landesdenkmalamt Berlin); German co-chair of the advisory board)
Dipl.-Rest. Gereon Lindlar, consultant and restoration expert, Bonn
Prof. Dr. Ines Weizman, Bauhaus-Universität Weimar
Dr.-Ing. Dietlinde Schmitt-Vollmer, University of Stuttgart, Institute of Architectural History
Christian Blatt, University of Stuttgart, Institute of Construction Materials
Menachem Leiba, chief executive officer, Municipality of Tel Aviv-Yafo
Ronit Ferber, head of the Community and Culture administration, Municipality of Tel Aviv-Yafo
Arik Shua, deputy head of the Community and Culture administration, Municipality of Tel Aviv-Yafo
Giyora Yahalom, head of the Arts and Culture department, Municipality of Tel Aviv-Yafo
Liran Ania, deputy head of the Arts and Culture department, Municipality of Tel Aviv-Yafo
Michal Linenberg, head of the Cultural Bialik Square, Arts and Culture department, Municipality of Tel Aviv-Yafo
Michal Keinan, chief development officer, Tel Aviv Foundation
Limor Ben Benisti, chief financial officer, Tel Aviv Foundation
Sarit Ben Or, finance account manager, Tel Aviv Foundation
Barbara Hendricks, former German federal building minister
Ron Huldai, mayor of Tel Aviv-Yafo
Friederike Zobel, head of International Thematic Focus Bauhaus 2019, Kulturstiftung des Bundes
Hortensia Völckers, artistic director, Kulturstiftung des Bundes
Alexander Farenholtz, administrative director, Kulturstiftung des Bundes

Thank you again for taking part in our journey,
Shira, Sharon, and Ellen

p. 75 ↑: photo © Gut-Mossinson Collection, Younes & Soraya Nazarian Library, University of Haifa
p. 75 ↓: © Eliyahu brothers postcard collection, courtesy of Dr. Dalia Levy-Eliyahu. Thank you to Vered Navon, author of “The Boulevard: Jerusalem Boulevard Through the Eyes of the Photographers.”
p. 76: The Tel Aviv-Yafo Municipality Archives
p. 78: cover page of the *News bulletin of the Tel Aviv city administration*, 1935
p. 80: Itzhak Kalter
p. 83 ↑: Central Zionist Archives, PHKH\1278840
p. 83 ↓: Ilan Karmi
p. 87 ↑: 3D rendering: Lõrincz Áron, photo: Aviad Bar Ness
p. 87 ↓: Amnon Bar Or Architects
S. 88: Nir Ovadia
p. 93: Brenne Architekten
p. 94 ↑: Itzhak Kalter, Karmi Archive
p. 94 ↓: Karmi Archive
pp. 96–102: Karmi Archive
p. 103: Courtesy of the State Archives of Israel
p. 106: Shula Widrich, courtesy of Michael Ofer
p. 109: private collection Daniella De-Nur
pp. 111–113: Shula Widrich, courtesy of the Scheuer family
p. 160 ↓: Yoram Aschheim
p. 162 ↑: Shani Nachmias
p. 162 ↓: private photo
p. 163 ↑: Guy Yechiely
p. 164 ↑: Stefanie von Becker
p. 164 ↓: Oliver Giese/Sto Foundation
p. 165 ↑: Alica Christ
p. 166 ↓: private photo

All other photos were taken by the fabulous Yael Schmidt, Tel Aviv.

An imprint of Walter de Gruyter GmbH, Berlin/Boston
Texts by kind permission of the authors.
Pictures by kind permission of the photographers/holders of the picture rights.

Editorial direction and interviews: Florian Heilmeyer, Katrin Voermanek
Photos (unless otherwise noted): Yael Schmidt
Translation: Michael Thomas Taylor (pp. 28–29, 32–50, 70–157)
Copyediting: Michael Thomas Taylor
Proofreading: Michael Thomas Taylor
Project management jovis: Theresa Hartherz
Production jovis: Susanne Rösler
Design and setting: Avi Bohbot, Gila Kaplan
Lithography: Bild1Druck
Printing and binding: Graspo

Bibliographic information published by the Deutsche Nationalbibliothek:
The Deutsche Nationalbibliothek lists this publication in the Deutsche Nationalbibliografie; detailed bibliographic data are available on the Internet at
http://dnb.d-nb.de.

jovis Verlag
Genthiner Straße 13
10785 Berlin

www.jovis.de

jovis books are available worldwide in select bookstores. Please contact your nearest bookseller or visit www.jovis.de for information concerning your local distribution.

ISBN 978-3-98612-021-4 (softcover)
ISBN 978-3-98612-025-2 (e-book)

Federal Ministry for Housing, Urban Development and Building